Dream Big - The Universe is Listening

Also by Ilona Selke

Wisdom of the Dolphins
Dolphins, Love and Destiny
Alin Learns to Use His Imagination

Dream Big

The Universe is Listening

Creating a Better World for Yourself and the Planet

Ilona Selke

Selke, Ilona
Dream Big - The Universe is Listening
Creating a Better Life for Yourself and the Planet

1. Personal Growth
2. Inspirational
I. Title II. Selke, Ilona
ISBN 978-1-884246-21-0

DEDICATION

Foremost and above all, I thank God for creation and for being endowed with consciousness. It is to the illumination of this spark of God with myself and each one of us, that I dedicate this book.

Table of Contents

GRATITUDE & ACKNOWLEDGMENTS

Looking back on my life I have to say that I am foremost thankful to all my teachers. My first, utterly meaningful teacher, was my mother. She knew that she was ahead of her time and she taught me early on how to get in touch with my inner voice, my inner sight and my inner wisdom. For this and so much more, I'm eternally grateful to my mother and even though she left planet Earth when I was only 23 years old, she is forever in my heart.

I thank all the teachers who supported me and believed in me. They may not know it but all the teachers who saw the spark of soul in me, starting in grammar school, through middle school, high school and into university, are regularly on my mind and in my heart.

And of course I'm utterly grateful to all the authors who took the time to sit and write down their wisdom and inspiration which shaped my mind and paved the path of who I was to become. If it wasn't for the teachers and the writers, I would not be the person I am today. This is also why I keep on keeping on. This is why I keep teaching, this is why I keep writing. When I look outside and look at the sunshine and the nature beckoning me, I keep writing because I hope to provide this kind of inspiration for others to climb the ladder into illumination themselves.

Beyond words of gratitude I am utterly grateful to my husband Don Paris. I do kiss the ground he walks on. Truly, it is through his assistance that I became the person who I am now. He was my meditation teacher when I came to study with him at age twenty one. After we discovered a mutual passion to help teach people, he stood by my side and helped me teach small groups and then later on to teach larger seminars. His love, his spiritual wisdom, his multidimensional being turns my everyday life into living in Heaven on Earth.

I thank him for having traveled the high road to God with me, which was the first words I heard him speak. For his love, romantic, erotic, emotional, mental and spiritual light, and his endurance and his belief in me. For his immensely wise guidance, his technical skills in our day to day life, from building our house to editing my books and films, his total surrender, and his absolute dedication to surrendering ourselves into the unity of the One.

I thank my sister Marion Selke and my niece Lena Drews who've been working with me in spreading *Living From Vision*®. My sister has been training LFV teachers and coaches for the last 25 years. My niece is now coaching people in how to live from vision, as she is a living example of a person who has consciously worked with these principles since birth. She is now co-authoring a book with me, titled **Living From Vision.**

I thank all my dear, dear friends who have taken eternal time to travel with me into the inner worlds, who have explored with me the dimensions that most people don't see. It is through these explorations that they have been my teachers as well. Don Paris, Bruce BecVar, Merlin Mueller, Amoraea, John Brierley, Juergen and Tanja Brehm, Bettine Clemen, John Burgos, Dr. John Murungi, Rocco D'Ordine, Shreanz Daga, Patriji, Lobsang Wangyal, Fernando and Carlos, Marion Selke with whom I traveled endless hours when we were sisters in our childhood years and Susanne Lampe-Osten in my teenage years, who both set the stage for my exploration of consciousness.

I also thank all the many seminar participants with whom I was able to eye gaze, and enter the dimensions of soul consciousness. Some of these meetings were utterly divine.

I thank the late Dr. Bob Beck, Dr. Vernon Woolf, Dr. Rod Newton as well as the late Dr. Willard Frank, for having been hugely instrumental in my life, to having set the stage to become a surfer in time-space, and to live in Heaven on Earth. Because of them, I have become the blossom of who I am now.

I thank Roberta Goodman and all the different dolphin researchers, but especially her, for her incredible inspirations and contributions to information about dolphin consciousness. And I thank all the dolphins who, with their loving presence, their sonar and their multidimensional presence, have shaped me and help me inspire so many people on this planet.

I'm filled to the brim with love and gratitude for all my Bali staff, currently 34 people and too many to name individually, who help run our *Shambala Spa* in Ubud and our *Shambala Retreat Center* on the north shore of Bali, for helping maintain a Heaven on Earth and a wellspring of rejuvenation and inspiration for all the visitors who come to visit us in Bali. I've learned to love the Bali culture through them and I've peeked into dimensions that I would have never, ever known without their help. I love their hugs, I love their dedication. Thank you from the bottom of my heart Made Arsa, Sri, Dewi, Edy, Putu Dharma Yasa, and Tika. And I equally thank all the group leaders who've brought amazing students to our Shambala Retreat Center as well as their own brilliance to help illuminate this world.

Thank you Beth and Andrew Sabo for holding up the mothership, our business, home and headquarters here in America, while we're traveling around the world to spread our work. It's because of your impeccability and dedication to awesomeness that we can do this.

I want to thank Han Ye and Wang Gang and Mr. Han in China for the incredible dedication to providing proof that scalar technology creates tangible results. You've awed my heart with your dedication to make a difference on this planet.

I thank the LFV team in Singapore for having relentlessly kept on teaching *Living From Vision*® in Singapore to the disadvantaged, the dropout kids, and to the corporate world.

I thank the late Cody Johnson and his wife Robin for having held the Prophet's Conferences and given me this stage amongst some of the great thought leaders and luminaries of our times. Thank you for having believed in me.

My gratitude also goes out to DNA Publishing, to Nick Nanton & his team, who opened the doors for me to meet with Brian Tracy as well as Jack Canfield and to be a co-author with both, as well as to be interviewed by Jack Canfield, co-author of Chicken Soup for the Soul.

I thank Jack Canfield for his quote, a man who truly works at making a difference here on this planet, and helping people help other people.

I thank Margot Anand, author of Sex, Love & Awakening and her international bestselling books on <u>tantra and ecstasy</u>. I thank her for her friendship! Such a brilliant, adventuresome soul, who opened the doors to Tantra here in the West. Thank you for your loving quote and friendship.

I thank all my Bali friends who make a rare and wild assortment of thought leaders, and co-creatives. Especially Sacha Stone from New Earth Haven, Ken Cooke, Noelle Simpson, Juan Schlosser, Frederik Stimmel, Mark Lee, and so many more!

I thank WASABI Publicity for their great vision and scope of expertise. Thank you for taking me under your wings.

I thank Trevor Crane for his out-of-the-box publishing techniques, getting me on the map and thank you for your guidance in the process of getting my book done and out to the world.

I also thank Lisa Lockwood for her coaching during my writing and publishing process.

Thank you Robyn Lynn for having been my writing buddy. Your words are so soul touching and deep!

Thank you Odette Singleton-Wards for having edited my book! It was such a pleasure, literally.

And lastly, thank you to all the amazing world-wide speakers at my DREAM BIG SUMMIT sharing about creating a better place for ourselves and the planet.

DREAM BIG

THE UNIVERSE IS LISTENING

INTRODUCTION

Yogis and quantum physicists alike, tell us that our 3-D life is not really solid, or even real. There is nothing here but vast empty space between atoms, which in and of themselves, seems to fluctuate in and out of existence.

Actually, quantum physics tells us that everything consists out of an oscillating quantum foam, which is turning ON and OFF at the rate of 50 billion times per second. For all we know, this could mean we might just be binary code.

Imagine this quantum foam being in existence and blinking out of existence 50,000,000,000 times per second. We would never notice when something wasn't there, because it goes by so fast. But this single concept alone, which emerging scientists and seers in the ancient past both have uttered, this single concept of something being there and not there will be your ticket to creating miracles.

Most of the people reading this book have probably already created a parking spot when and where they needed one. However, have you ever sat still long enough to consider the immensity of the concept that the universe is actually listening? The concept that the universe is connected to our innermost thoughts and feelings is staggering.

To think that the universe actually cares about what we hold in our innermost thoughts – we should be shouting about this from the rooftops!

But of course, to many people it doesn't seem that obvious anymore. Scientific thinking has eliminated the openness to consider that our thoughts affect reality.

Religions have proclaimed for millennia that this interactive conversation with God is real, but the teachings have been clothed in metaphors that seem outdated for most of us who have been raised in the Western civilization. Scientific thinking has taken over. We don't really have a valid model for such an amazing universe that does listen to our thoughts and feelings.

Einstein once said that he didn't believe that God is playing dice with our universe, however he had to concede that there was such a thing as "spooky action at a distance."

Our digital world and our quantum scientists have meanwhile given us possible metaphors to understand that life is not quite what it seems and is not as solid as it appears at times.

By reading this book, I will reveal to you how real this magical universe is, how much our thoughts and innermost feelings do matter, and how you can set up this communication to "God", the "Center of the Universe" or whatever else you may wish to call it, even more effectively.

I will provide you with real life stories that will allow you to entrain your conscious and subconscious mind with new beliefs of what is possible.

We can all live in a universe that plays to a higher tune. Much of what we consider to be real is largely a reflection of what we've been taught to accept as possible.

I will share stories of miracles, as well as steps you can take with you, that I and others have experienced to help broaden our collective concept as to what is possible.

We are definitely at a crossroads here. If we keep going in the direction of the logical mindset, applying only our rational mind, we may walk ourselves into extinction. Our scientific world is taking us towards a much more materialistic worldview. There is the belief that we can transfer consciousness into a computer, as trans-humanists believe. Robotics is on the rise. But if we keep going in that direction, who will be there to teach our children that you can link with your eyes and have miracles happen? Where will the shamans be? Where will the rishis, the seers of old India, and the yogis be – those who showed many of us the way?

On the other hand, some scientists like Elon Musk, the inventor of the Tesla vehicle, PayPal, and SpaceX space program, believe that we are living in a simulation. Recently, newspapers have been filled with articles that state that scientists feel that we are living in a hologram. Life may well be more like *The Matrix*, if you are awake enough.

This is great news! If you can wake up enough to the higher laws of the universe, you have the opportunity to jump in between the worm-holes of time and space and learn how to shift into one of the many parallel universes of your choice. Ultimately, to jump out and beyond the world of appearances, into full-on illumination.

If you can develop the ability to enter in between the space of atoms, it can allow you to wake up beyond the daily drudgery of reacting to what comes at you. It will allow you to express yourself truly as the highest possible expression which you are meant to be.

Applied to your daily life, it may mean that if something in your life is not working out, you simply rerun the movie, and recalibrate your dream. I will write stories that are dramatic enough to make you wonder if it could even be real. And yes, everything I have written is true.

As you know, daily life has very real ups and downs. Life pulls on our emotions, pulls on our attention and we at times find ourselves dragged down instead of being able to lift our heads above the clouds.

And this is what we have to learn; to walk with our heads above the clouds and with our feet on the ground in order to dream up a new dream.

What is it then that the yogis, the sages of the ages and the enlightened ones can impart to us?

We are living in a modern world, but we are not that different to any sentient being, whether aborigines in Australia or East Indian yogis of India.

The Dreaming Mind has been used as an allegory, a metaphor by humans in ancient and modern times. Until recently, the Aborigines in Australia used their dreaming mind to find waterholes, to communicate at a distance and to use the dreaming mind to survive. Aborigines used to bring about a desired outcome by utilizing the power of the puri-puri images which they painted onto

17

rock walls. These were images that depicted the desired outcome of a situation. This is not all that different from the teachings that were proclaimed in the book **_The Secret_**.

All of us are capable of communicating with every part of life! We all can be fully awake. The universe is always listening to each and every one of us, all the time.

We are multidimensional beings, whether we are aware of it or not. I will show you enough evidence so that you can come to trust in this multidimensional universe.

To create a more fulfilled life we simply need to ask for what we really want.

Knock on the door of the universe and we will be given the answers. As we become more aware, we discover the power of our consciousness and how it interacts with the outer world.

The purpose of this book is to show you exactly how to manifest and surf the waves of time-space. How to live in Heaven whilst on Earth, and how to reach into states of enlightenment – touching the face of God – while you live in this lifetime.

Everything I write about is true, and I have put it all to the test during the last thirty years. Everything I speak about, every story I write about, is true. The only things I've altered are some of the names or descriptions of people so as not to reveal their identity.

With this, I wish you the greatest of adventures into the miraculous, and living as a luminous and enlightened being here on Earth.

INDIA

MAGIC OR MIRACLES

I was sitting on the cool stone floor in an *ashram* in India. We had left our shoes outside the big door, were sitting cross-legged with our eyes closed, singing devotional songs, called chanting mantras or *bhajans*. Incense wafted through the air and candles were lit, creating an atmosphere of wonder.

An *ashram* is a monastery type place usually run by a *guru* in residence, open to all spiritual seekers. Our group leader had told us that if we were really lucky the baba at this ashram would manifest a piece of jewelry to one member of our group.

Don and I were sitting in the last row in the hall against the wall, giving the priority seating to our Japanese co-travelers, as they were very eager to see some magical feats. They really wanted to fan their faith and their belief in a higher power.

We had chosen to sit far from the podium, far from where the baba (meaning father) was to take his seat. I didn't want to draw any attention to myself. He was due to make his appearance and manifest ashes right from his otherwise empty hands.

I wasn't completely convinced about this type of manifestation-miracle stuff. Maybe I wasn't ready to accept these out-of-this-world manifestation miracles which India was famous for. And maybe my disbelief said more about the lowly status of my ignorance, but something just didn't feel right to me about it.

While the baba was getting ready behind the scenes in the back room, we all sang bhajans in the big meditation hall. Singing devotional songs was designed to open our hearts for the meeting.

Closing my eyes, I gently slipped into meditation while the chanting around me grew in pitch. The wafting plumes of incense truly had transported me into a different world. In my mind I was seeing this baba prepare a black star sapphire ring in the back room. In my reverie he told me in clear terms, "I am going to pick *you* today and manifest this black sapphire ring *for you!*"

Since I don't really like black as a color, I asked him in my reverie if he could change the ring to a blue star sapphire ring.

Was this communication wishful thinking, I wondered, *or was it real?*

Soon the baba came out of his cloistered room and started to walk slowly through the rows of people sitting on the floor. It was just like in the movies. As he walked through the rows like perhaps the pope would stride, his adherent believers and seekers were eager to touch his feet, or at least touch the seam of his long robe as he passed them by.

Eyes were riveted on his rubbing fingers, as everyone knew he was about to materialize holy ash in his hands. This holy ash is also called *vibuti*. Indeed, lo and behold, the ashes started to flow out of his bare hands. This was one of the miracles that many had waited to see with their own eyes.

As he passed through the rows of devoted seekers, he anointed people's foreheads with this holy ash as it kept flowing out. Giving this ash anointment was a blessing which reminded me of the blessing people receive in the Catholic Church on Ash Wednesday. (*Ash Wednesday* opens Lent, a season of fasting and prayer. *Ash Wednesday* takes place 46 days before Easter Sunday.)

I really was not a fan of these kinds of miracles which was why Don and I had taken our place at the back of the hall. We wanted to hide behind the many Japanese and Indians who had come to be awed.

Hopefully he won't pick me! I prayed.

Just as he sat down on his divan on the slightly elevated podium, he pointed his hands in my direction and motioned for me to come to the front of the hall. That is the moment when you want to say "Me?" while turning around and checking behind your back, hoping that he had summoned someone else.

Well, it was indeed me he wanted and I walked to the front of the hall, slightly dreading this moment. I kneeled before him and offered my respects. I didn't want to make a spectacle, so I just went along with what I thought was a show.

However, for everyone else this was the moment they had all been waiting for. Holding their breath, with silent drum rolls in their minds, they watched the baba swirl his arms! After a few magical circling movements of his hands, reminding me of a magician on stage, the baba opened his hand and proudly presented a black star sapphire ring as a manifestation gift to me.

It was just like he had told me in my mind a little earlier. I stared at the black sapphire ring, not knowing what to believe. I could practically hear everyone gasp. I stared at the ring and instantly used my logical mind to discount all possible ways that this was a genuine miracle.

This type of manifestation reminded me of snake charmers; a trick. I have to admit, I could not say with 100% certainty that this manifestation was truly fake.

And to be honest, I know full well, that in order to arrive at a new destination and to discover new horizons, one has to keep an open mind. Columbus, though not the first, would not have discovered America and disproven the Flat Earth theory to the predominant mindset at his time if he had believed in what the status quo was saying. We *do* need to learn to think out of the box to reach new shores. But today I had to admit to myself, that this manifestation was just a bit too much out of my own box, so that I preferred to pass it off as a magic trick.

I knew that in order to discover the hidden worlds, one has to begin with an open mind. But today, watching this kind of manifestation just smacked of trickery to me.

For example, so I reasoned, the baba had told me in my mind that he was going to manifest a black sapphire ring for me. In my mind I had seen him get ready in the back room. If he had not prepared something ahead of time, so I thought, he could not have spoken like that with me in my mind.

The fact that I saw him get ready behind the scenes, albeit only in my inner mind, and telling me ahead of time, telepathically, that he was going to pick me out of the group, which turned out to be true, and then to actually 'manifest' a black star sapphire ring after all, all these points left me with the lingering feeling that it was just a good and well planned show.

This baba was an imitation of the famous and renowned Sathya Sai Baba whom I had read about years back, when I was seventeen years old. I was mystified and caught between fascination and doubt. Nevertheless, I kept reading books and stories about the magical **Masters of the Far East**. I read about the power of the third eye, which gives one the ability to know the past and the future.

I had heard about yogis who manifested flowers in their open palms. I had read about the Philippine healers who performed operations with their bare hands as if the body was a mere illusion. I was riveted and really wanted to know what the secret laws of the universe were. I did want to venture out and discover a world and dimension beyond the ordinary. *"Fly with the eagles or scratch with the chickens"* was a motto that had stuck with me.

It was the first time I had seen such a magical manifestation right before my own eyes and I must admit, I was not very willing to believe that these "out of this world" manifestations were really real.

However, I was amazed to notice how many participants in our little travel group were now willing to believe in God.

The miracles that the baba performed were not meaningful in and of themselves. They were meant to be a demonstration of a power that exists in our universe that is beyond what meets the eye.

The eyes of some of our Japanese participants grew filled with light, awe and wonder. The miracle gave them the belief and certainty that higher powers were at work in the universe, a higher power other than which regular school had taught them.

We hold beliefs as to what is possible as a collective truth, either as a family, as a group, as a society, or as a nation.

We reiterate these truths, and can't do anything more than what the sum beliefs of our peer group that we belong to, can hold.

Shamans used to live outside of the village boundaries, and they were able and allowed to do things which defied the natural laws of physics as we know them.

I know that witnessing miracles can be very helpful to stretch our limiting beliefs. But in the end, what all the miracles point to is one truth: That we are living in a universe that is far, far different than what we are led to believe.

The Japanese participants took this manifestation as real, and this gave them the certainty that we are indeed living in a matrix, a universe that is listening to our thoughts very closely.

But how can we personally get access to such greatness, to being able to live outside the constraints of ordinary living? How can we get out of the box? Just knowing about it is not enough.

But let me tell you how I had gotten into this ashram.

BORN IN THE HIMALAYAS

I was born in the Himalayas to German parents who had been living in the Middle and Far East for some years before I was born. During the first three months that my mom was pregnant with me, my parents were traveling through India. To add to the mystery of my life, my mother always told me that she had picked up my soul from India.

During my childhood, my mother told me many tales from the Middle and Far East. Since we lived in the Himalayas during the first three years of my life, these stories seemed all the more real to me. My mother had been inspired by the spiritual teachings of India, before the hippies made yoga and meditation popular. She taught me yoga and meditation from when I was five years old.

Reading the miraculous stories of Aladdin from the book of ***One Thousand and One Nights*** got my imagination going. The young Aladdin had discovered a secret to manifesting. The ability to manifest things out of thin air mesmerized my young mind and stirred an ancient memory in me that such things are our divine birthright. Beyond that, Aladdin and his princess had captivated my heart, and I vividly imagined living the life of Aladdin and his princess in a colorful palace.

During the same time period that Aladdin had captured my attention, my mother taught me yoga postures and meditation.

I recall the day she taught me the Yogic Breath, where

you hold one nostril closed while either inhaling or exhaling through the other for a steady count. She told me to look at the root of my nose. There she told me to watch for a small bright light or a flame.

But no matter how much I stared into my inner mind, there was only solid blackness to be found. I could not see a light, try as I might. The canvas of my inner mind remained pitch black. At night however, while going to sleep, I floated out into the stars and I felt at once captivated by this strange weightlessness. I experienced myself floating and tilting in this huge universe. But I could not make heads or tails out of my nightly adventures.

My mom never had a TV at our home and to this day I still don't have one, but my grandparents did. So I did get to indulge in a few life-forming television shows. One of them was the TV Show **I Dream of Jeannie** which I was able to watch weekly at my grandparents' home.

It is a story of a real genie that had been contained in a bottle for over 2000 years and fell in love with a stranded astronaut who had landed from outer space on a deserted island. The genie was from the Far East, dressed in a beautiful Arabic-Indian costume and simply had to fold her arms and blink her eyes to create miracles. This set the theme for my young mind. This is when I got immersed in the quest to find out how to manifest with my thoughts.

How exactly can people manifest by just having a wish or an idea? I wondered. I needed to find out. I constantly observed my thoughts, and over time noticed that I often got exactly what I didn't want.

It was the beginning of seeing proof that we live in an interactive universe. At least it was a proof that I was going to be put to the test. That will be another story later on, where I will describe to you how I set up this rigorous test of how our thoughts manifest reality here on planet Earth, at the ripe old age of 10 years old. It was a milestone when I discovered that my universe was actually listening.

While I was mesmerized by images of various genies, my mother focused on teaching me the more profound things of life.

We typically spent our vacations at a farm in the hilly, northern part of Germany. During one of our daily hikes through a pine tree forest my mother asked me to stand still and listen to the silence of the forest.

I stood still in order to be able to hear more clearly and strained my little ears to hear the sound of silence. I listened and listened, but all I could hear was the wind blowing lightly, but most of all I heard nothing. For the world, I could not hear anything more. *Silence must have a very special sound*, I reasoned, *beyond my abilities*.

My mother's teachings set the tone for my inner development. My mom took the example of listening to the silence of the forest to set the stage to listen to something even more refined. She taught me how to listen to the voice of my consciousness, to the voice of my heart and my conscience. By listening more attentively to sounds, even the sounds of silence, the deeper voices of our inner being come more to the foreground. This is what she was really trying to get me to listen to.

Just like a true master teaches his or her student, so my mom asked me to listen to the voice within and to follow my own inner light.

This training took time. Teaching ethics to children is a lengthy process. Instead of telling me what was right and what was wrong, or telling me what to do, she taught me the most valuable gift: To discern from right and wrong by listening to the voice of my heart.

I knew early on, in my teenage years, when most teenagers try to rebel against authority, that I didn't have to fight. There was no authority to tell me what to do, just my mom who had taught me to listen to my inner heart and mind.

I didn't want to smoke or get drunk just because everyone else did. My inner voice was getting louder and clearer and told me what to stay away from. I knew that Coca-Cola was off my list. I told doctors not to prescribe any antibiotics for me. Where on Earth did I get this wisdom from? Surely my mom's teaching of tuning into my inner wisdom was the key.

It was not the dogma that I was taught to follow, but instead my mom taught me to develop my own intuition. This gift built the foundation for my entire life, one that I keep teaching in my teachings now. If you have children or grandchildren, try to imagine ways to help the child discover their own inner wisdom. I have published children's books in Hindi, English, German, Polish, and Russian to teach children how to "tune in." Guided imagery journeys guide the children to "listen within." The children that were taught these methods throughout their childhood and worked with my children's book techniques have now become radiant adults. They learned how to listen to a higher tune. They didn't need to fight but rather have used their talents to be greater gifts to society.

"There is much more between Heaven and Earth than meets the eye," were my grandfather's words many times. His words still come to my mind again and again. He always told me that much can be found between Heaven and Earth that we may never understand.

He told me how he was able to find water by dowsing, like a water-witcher – he was able to find water wells with just the use of a wooden forked branch. He simply walked over land, grasping this forked wooden branch in both of his hands, and when he came across a well or a water line, the wooden fork bent down to the ground. The more water there was, the harder the fork pulled down.

He also amazed me because he knew ahead of time who was going to come to our house, in plenty of time before they actually arrived. He would open the gates just in time for their car to pull in.

I was sixteen when my mom gave me the book **_Siddhartha_** by Hermann Hesse.

This book tells about the spiritual journey of a young boy, Siddhartha, the same as Buddha's name, before Buddha left the palace to become a renunciate. The boy in Hermann Hesse's book was seeking spiritual illumination. The deep wisdom from this book touched a chord in me and set me on the path of discovering the deeper truths of life.

When I was 18, on my first trip to the USA, I bought the book the ***Autobiography of a Yogi*** by Paramahansa Yogananda in the first New Age bookstore I ever set foot in. This world-famous book has helped millions of westerners find their way to meditation and awareness of their Soul.

It completely captured my heart and soul. Yogananda was deeply devoted to find God's light and the eternal truth and to share his adherent desire to serve. He wanted to be a divine light and to stimulate others to believe in the greatness of the universe. His miracle stories all serve to demonstrate only that goal. His tales of magic and miracles inspired me to no end and it helped set my life in the direction of finding out about what lay beyond the limits of our human consciousness and ordinary time-space.

Fast forward to 1996 to find out why we had been invited on our first India trip.

Don and I had just taught an SE-5 Seminar in Japan about Radionics and the SE-5 (a real miracle instrument http://www.SE-5.com). This instrument replaces the wooden sticks with which my grandfather used to be able to find water. It is a supreme dowsing instrument. Later I will tell you how much more miraculous it is. But back to our Japan story.

The organizer of our Japan seminars was a renowned author in Japan. He had invited Don and I to accompany his group of Japanese students on a pilgrimage to various renowned babas in India.

In preparation for this trip, our Japanese group leader

had given us videos of previously filmed miracles. We were able to convince ourselves by watching close-up footage of instantaneous healings, all filmed in slow motion. This footage left no doubt of the truth of such miracles. We saw close-up footage of Philippine healers, of Indian sages, and babas. Intrigued and wishing to fulfill a teenage desire to see these kinds of babas, we agreed to come along on the trip to India. We left with a group of orderly Japanese on a journey that was going to take us to visit many ashrams and meet many sages.

All the Japanese students were hoping to see real miracles and extraordinary manifestations. We were told that we would see ashes and jewels appear out of nowhere, right in front of our own eyes.

Yet the day that the baba manifested a black star sapphire ring for me did not have me completely convinced.

Manifestation and spiritual evolution – how did they fit together? Were miracles something of a lesser nature?

Luckily the next day, in another ashram, this time built like a pyramid, brought me greater insight.

A MASTER'S AURA

A more profound experience awaited us when we were invited to meditate in a pitch black pyramid in Kurnool, India. The visit to this pyramid was not on the program, but came about because of a recommendation of a Japanese friend of ours.

When our Japanese group of about twenty people arrived at the Pyramid Center, we were told that the *master* of this small ashram was not present today. The year before, the guru of this ashram had gone through a year of silence and had not addressed the previous Japanese group last year either.

To our delight, we were told that we all could enjoy the unique experience of meditating in this special pyramid instead. A few Indians were milling around, looking like they had been practicing meditation for some time. Soon our group filed into the dark pyramid and we took our seats in the far left corner. From the outside, the pyramid looked to be about 20 by 20 meters, but from the inside it was just a vast cave, pitch black.

As soon as everyone had settled in, it became evident that this pyramid – with only small slits for ventilation – was more like a sauna. Close to 100 degrees Fahrenheit we slowly started sweating.

To my delight, someone was starting to play the flute to lift our spirits. Riding on the sound current of the flute, I was lifted into higher worlds and enjoyed the extra help. Higher and higher I rose, through the eye of the needle into a state beyond time and space. If I were to put it into words or describe it as an image, I would describe it like this:

There was a masterful being that was pulling all the souls of our group up and out of the center opening at the top of the pyramid, as if through the eye of the needle, into a state beyond time or space.

I could see Don arriving on the other side of this pin-hole-of-a-needle-pathway as well. The masterful being who was playing the flute mentally told me to help pull others up and through this vortex of singularity.

I reveled in this moment of bliss and felt that this was the India of my heart. Albeit in a pyramid, I loved sitting in focused stillness and the ascension of soul awareness with others who could do the same.

As I was sitting in deep absorption, I kept rising into finer and finer vistas.

Suddenly, I was jolted by a wave of energy, which nearly made me bend backwards. Startled, I instantly opened my eyes! What I saw was astounding. About ten feet before me, right from where the flute player was sitting, I saw a brilliant golden aura surrounding this man's upper chest and head.

Mind you, it was very dark in the pyramid. With my eyes open I was now seeing this glowing golden light surrounding this being. Instantly the words burst out of my mind: *This being is mentally enlightened!*

I was breathless to witness such a miracle. I had seen some auras before in my life, but none like this.

Receiving this jolt of a current and seeing this glowing aura in the midst of no light whatsoever was breathtaking.

Quickly I realized that this golden aura was indeed coming from the flute player and I vowed to check later who this person was.

As the flute sounds quieted and the meditation came to an end, we were ushered out of the pyramid. The outside air was a relief to the sweltering hot air inside. We were all guided to take our seat on sandy grounds, beneath the blessed shade of some trees. To my amazement the flute player was actually the *master* of this ashram, simply called Patriji. There was no kissing the robe, no to-do. Nothing. He was humorous, and with his flowing white beard and white hair he looked like a classic image of a guru.

Fortunately he was willing to give us time for questions and answers. I was riveted and listened intently to what he had to say. This is how I liked it. The introduction had been done based on the merits of inner communion, not on the merit of a show.

He addressed all the seekers of our Japanese group as "Masters." He said, "If you want to get somewhere you have to assume the state of having arrived there already. Otherwise you will keep identifying with the space of being a seeker forever."

When faced with the question of what he thought about instantaneous manifestations – which we had witnessed on this tour plentifully by now – he laughed.

With a deep wisdom in his voice he told us, "Those manifestations are for show, trying to attract the masses.

A true yogi can do greater miracles, but only when there is a true need!"

Not only did he glow in the dark, gave me a jolt over a distance and gave wise words of wisdom, but I found out later he also had taken note of who in the group was alert and awake. Despite the pitch blackness inside, without any visible light to let him know who was who (no pun intended) he took note.

As we all said good bye, we received a personal hand-shake from Patriji. He told us to go and make sure we taught meditation. Don had been teaching meditation for years, and if you recall from my other books, Don was first my meditation teacher in 1983 while I was studying philosophy.

Don and I asked Patriji how we could make a donation. We had noticed that he had not once asked to be given money at all, which really impressed us. He replied with the most surprising answer, and said, "Go out and teach meditation! That will be the biggest help!"

A true master! I thought to myself.

He demonstrates no needs, he ignites others when no one is looking, has no need for fame, and he sees the *master* in everyone. He wants people to see their future fulfilled and see themselves as masterful beings thereby applying *"The Secret"* method to spiritual evolution.

Over the coming two decades this small pyramid cen-ter grew into the new Pyramid Valley Ashram called the *The Maitreya-Buddha Pyramid*, near Bangalore, attracting millions of followers and over 10,000 pyramid centers all over India and around the world. His students call him Patriji, but his title is Bramarshi Patriji.

Meditation, manifestations, miracles and magic! We found it all here in India. The questions: what is true spirituality, how do we evolve our soul, and what place does the power to heal and the power to manifest play in the path of our soul's evolution, were running through my heart and mind.

And most of all, I still wanted to know: "Is there only one reality or are there parallel realities? Is time and space fixed? Do we have destiny or free will, and if so why?"

But why India?

WHY INDIA?

Go confidently in the direction of your dreams.
Live the life you have imagined.
If you have built castles in the air, your work need not be lost; that is
where they should be. Now put the foundations under them.
This world is but a canvas to our imagination.
It's not what you look at that matters, it's what you see.
David Henry Thoreau

You might have read about the Findhorn Foundation, an eco-village and spiritual training center located in Scotland. I had heard about it when I was a teenager. At Findhorn they were able to grow pumpkins to gigantic sizes. But this was not done by giving more fertilizers, but simply by utilizing the power of prayer and positive thoughts. Instead of giving the plants chemicals to grow, they were talking to the plants to make them grow larger. And that was back in the seventies.

This inner communion made the plants magically grow bigger. This "nearly too good-to-be-true" story stayed with me my entire life. It is the stories of miracles that stay in our minds. I guess that is why Jesus used metaphors and stories to teach. We all still remember them today.

Stories are like a carrot in front of our monkey mind, they get our mind to expand and rise to greater vistas than we might have ordinarily explored.

There is a book with equally magical stories, called ***The Life and Teaching of the Masters of the Far East***. According to Wikipedia it has been a book that has played an

37

important part in introducing knowledge of the *masters* to the Western World, *masters* who are assisting and guiding the destiny of mankind.

I was fascinated by the miracles that these stories told about. And all that could happen if we managed to open our third eye.

Then there were tales about a place called Shangrila or Shambala. These stories spoke of a mystical space usually thought to be in the Himalayas, shrouded in secrets, describing tales of what is possible for us to experience here on Earth. These tales kept luring me to find this supernatural world.

Shambala is thought to be a place where beings of a higher order live together, located in the deep recesses of the Himalayan Mountains. The beings who live in Shambala defy the laws of normal physics, as they are living by a higher law, having learned how to affect time and space with their consciousness. Their vibrations are so fine that regular laws of physics do not apply to beings of this magnitude.

Even Newtonian laws are replaced by laws which only apply to beings of greater consciousness. In Shambala, thoughts are said to be able to manifest so quickly that it appears its inhabitants are living in a celestial world, right here on Earth. Indeed living in Heaven on Earth is what I wanted to find.

Stories of mysterious powers continuously capture the imagination of children and adults all the same. The books about Harry Potter have fascinated children and adults. Miracles, magic, defying the laws of physics, living by the power of the imagination, those are all speaking to a deeper knowing that there is a world that awaits us.

I wanted to find such magic and find out how to do it myself. Many years of adherent research and diligent practice has opened such a miraculous world.

Let me take you on a journey of such a magical quest for hidden mysteries and knowledge.

I took this magical journey over the last five decades to find Heaven on Earth, to find Shambala and to discover the hidden laws of the universe that make miracles happen.

Let me take you through stories that reveal the secret workings of the universe, in real life events. Each story shares a miracle of sorts and also a description of how to understand the unseen laws at work and how to utilize them in your life.

Let me show you how to find your own way through the maze of the art of manifestation and the art of your soul's evolution.

MANIFESTING A BICYCLE

I stared at the asphalt while walking on my way to school in order to focus my mind better. Inwardly I delivered my prayer to the universe. "I don't want a bike! I really don't want a bicycle. Please universe, here listening, please don't deliver a bicycle to me for Christmas!" I repeated these words silently to myself, much like a mantra. I was sure that the universe was eagerly listening.

I was about ten years old and I had already observed *that everything which I didn't want were the things that manifested.* Pondering the hidden laws of the universe as a youngster, I was a scientist at work. The more I observe my thesis, the more I saw the proof. This Christmas was going to be my final test to the universe. A light bulb had gone off in my innocent mind and I was sure that I had discovered a profound law of the universe which went like this: "Whatever I don't want, comes about!"

Since Christmas was just a few months away, I thought I could test my theory. I focused on NOT wanting a new bicycle. If I could somehow convince the universe that I didn't want a bicycle, then for sure I would get the bicycle, according to my newly discovered RULE #1 of the universe.

I had already repeated this experiment several times on smaller things and this Christmas experiment was going to be my final proof.

Christmas came closer and closer and my excitement grew! To this day I recall the moment I was to be given my Christmas gift. In Germany, Christmas is celebrated on the 24th, Christmas Eve. We had finished our dinner and with holy rapture we sang Christmas carols beside our candlelit Christmas tree. Unable to wrap up a bicycle in paper, my mother had placed my brand new bicycle behind the curtains in the living room. And now I was told to check behind the curtains for my Christmas gift. I was sure that the bicycle I had asked the universe not to deliver to me, had been delivered. And it was! My discovered law of the universe had found its final proof.

Now I was sure that the universe was listening! The RULE #1 for manifestation in my youthful scientific research had proven to be correct. If we were to imagine what we didn't want for long enough, the universe that is always listening would eventually give us what we didn't want.

We all know from personal experience that there is a sort of truth about this discovery. It is not that we get what we don't want, but that we get what we focus on, especially if we have some kind of emotion attached.

When you think of something you don't want, it's impossible not to imagine it. Try to imagine a *no-bicycle.* The universe, nor our subconscious does not understand a NO or a NOT.

Try this for example: Try not to think of a pink elephant. Voila, there is your pink elephant in your mind! It didn't help that I told you not to think about it.

The universe conversely responds to our thoughts and feelings: **What we focus on is what we get.** It doesn't matter whether we are imagining something that we are trying to get away from, or focusing in a positive way on something that we wish for. We get what we focus on. And the more emotions we have invested in it, the faster the manifestation.

I know that you do not want to consciously create anything unpleasant. But let me ask you, how often do you run a sad soap opera in your mind? How often do you run the negative outcome movie of your life or an experience through your mind? How often do you speak in jest, using sarcasm of exactly the opposite of what you wish to experience or have?

Let me remind you here: We constantly create, whether it is consciously or unconsciously done.

Whatever is in our subconscious or conscious or super-conscious mind, our thoughts and feelings constantly create a blueprint for what is to come, one hundred percent of the time. The beliefs we took on as children, the beliefs the people around us hold, everything influences our mind.

Luckily most of the time our thoughts are not focused like a laser beam of light, otherwise our thoughts and feelings would manifest instantly.

Like a 100 Watt light bulb can light up a small area to read a book by at night, or it can be focused as a laser light, meaning all the light is focused in the same direction and even just 100 Watts can cut steel or reach the moon.

The coherency factor of our thoughts determines the speed of their manifestation. If the coherency is low, the results are slow. Incoherent thoughts are unfocussed thought, going here and there, jumping around like a monkey, from idea to idea. Coherency is created by having one single focus and one single outcome in mind. When such a thought is backed by feelings, and the feeling of 100% certainty sets in, then the energy of our thoughts are streamlined, like a laser light and can reach the moon.

All our thoughts and feelings, even our unconscious beliefs, create results. Either slowly or quickly, consciously or unconsciously, depending on our coherency.

I was happy that I had figured out that *the universe was listening*. And I knew how I had to talk to it.

Since I had created a way of manifesting what I wanted, even when it looked like I only got what I didn't want, I felt on top of the world. In the end, I now knew how to get what I wanted.

Unfortunately we also get what we have focused on when we least expect it. TV shows and movies provide much food for our unconscious desires, for the better or worse, which the universe sets out to manifest, whether we want it or not.

Let me tell you how I found my first husband, how I suffered despite the deep love and then how I manifested my *soulmate*.

HOW TO FIND YOUR SOULMATE

Unending Love

I seem to have loved you in numberless forms, numberless times...
In life after life, in age after age, forever.
My spellbound heart has made and remade the necklace of songs,
That you take as a gift, wear round your neck in your many forms,
In life after life, in age after age, forever.

Whenever I hear old chronicles of love, its age-old pain,
Its ancient tale of being apart or together.
As I stare on and on into the past, in the end you emerge,
Clad in the light of a pole-star, piercing the darkness of time:
You become an image of what is remembered forever.

You and I have floated here on the stream that brings from the fount.
At the heart of time, love of one for another.
We have played alongside millions of lovers,
Shared in the same shy sweetness of meeting,
the distressful tears of farewell,
Old love but in shapes that renew and renew forever.

Today it is heaped at your feet, it has found its end in you
The love of all man's days both past and forever:
Universal joy, universal sorrow, universal life.
The memories of all loves merging with this one love of ours –
And the songs of every poet past and forever.

Rabindranath Tagore, Selected Poems

I had just turned 17 and was still living in Germany,
going to the gymnasium to get my Abitur, an equivalent

of an AA in America. It was 1978, and our summer break had arrived.

For my vacation, my girlfriend and I had taken a bicycle tour through Belgium, trotting from youth hostel to youth hostel. I was reading the book **Siddhartha** by Hermann Hesse, a prosaic rendition of the life of Gautama Buddha. On this trip I had found the perfect youth hostel. It was situated right on the Meuse River, a totally alternative youth hostel, where we were woken up by classical music in the morning.

The patron of the house hand-cooked breakfast for everybody personally and he was in need for extra staff to help him clean and run the youth hostel. The day I arrived back home from my magical summer trip, I turned right around and went back. The train dropped me off at the Namur main train station and I walked to the youth hostel by the river with a backpack on my back.

I remember the very moment when I looked at the old quaint house, now turned youth hostel. Standing behind the large glass window by the reception was the tall young man, standing like a solemn captain, with his arms folded across his chest, looking straight out of the windows, and straight at me.

He was the matching image of one of my TV heroes, *The Rifleman* and therefore it was love at first sight. I walked into the hostel to register and saw that he was still looking at me. The next morning, the young man woke us up with the gentle classical music of *"Pachelbel's Canon."* What a romantic wake-up call that wafted through the house!

Playing games like Mastermind, we soon discovered that we were able to read each other's minds with great ease. He was deep, he was dear, and we fell in love. He gave up his plans to return to the US and moved with me to Germany where I was finishing school. Before I had turned 19 years old, he steered me towards the most spiritual books that deeply influenced my life. When I was 20 years old, we eloped to get married and moved to the United States so that we could both study at university.

However, soon I discovered – much to my dismay – that he did not share my desire to meditate despite the fact that he had introduced me to pivotal spiritual books in my life. We didn't match in our sexual needs either. Despite the fact that he had matched my image of my dream man from the TV show *The Rifleman*, I was increasingly frustrated by his apparent lack and interest to merge with me on these important levels. For whatever reason, he rather wanted to live in a sort of solitude. It was as if he had been a monk in another lifetime and was having a hard time adjusting to modern values and joys.

But as you know it's only when we take 100% responsibility first, and own our creations, that we have the ability to create a better life.

To his defense, not blaming him for his lack of sexual interest, I have to let you in on a secret. This will show you how our often subconscious beliefs and values create the life around us. We might feel like blaming the others, but in reality they are simply doing a fine job at mirroring our inner beliefs, values, and pains.

When I was 16 years old, after an unfortunate ending

of a love affair with an Israeli young man, I was heartbroken and had decided that I clearly needed to focus on my spiritual life and put sexuality on hold.

I had judged myself as being too sexual at the end of that love story gone awry, which formed the foundation of my solemn vow – not to be sexual that quickly – ever again.

This was the vow: A man wishing to become my boyfriend would have to wait at least 6 weeks before I would be sexual with him.

Please remember these were the seventies, and six weeks of waiting was a long, long time in my mind. But deeper than the time limit which I had put on a man wanting to merge with me, I had made an emotional change within myself.

My judgment against my own sexuality created a belief that scarcity was better for me. And as you know whatever deep feeling or beliefs we carry within us, we will eventually find the match in our outside world.

I was looking for a match to my newly treasured values, unbeknownst to me. Consciously we may wish for something else, but the universe listens to our inner tune, our deeper subconscious thoughts and images much more.

Our beliefs become the invisible blueprints and architectural designs for our outer circumstances. These blueprints are literally thought holograms, which resonate out into the universe. And in turn, the universe responds and finds the perfect match.

I'm sure you're not too surprised to hear that the man I picked perfectly reflected the judgment I had made within myself. And so it came that Rick was not that interested in sex. Although he did not advertise this attitude and belief on his forehead when we met, every fiber of me must have known. He was a perfect match to my deeper beliefs which I had developed. And yes he was willing to wait six weeks. I think that should've been a dead giveaway.

Although it does help to have a list of characteristics we wish to see in our partner, and we may well get them, we will also receive the match to our unconsciously held beliefs and feelings.

I did have such a small list of preferred attributes and Rick fulfilled at least one of those consciously chosen items from my list. My husband-to-be had to speak English. The TV series *The Rifleman* had set the ideal image in my mind and he matched that image.

It wasn't the only image that I held in my mind. Another one was Winnetou, a character from Karl May stories about white Americans encountering Native Americans. Played by Pierre Brice, with his long black hair, he was the epitome of a beautiful man to me. But first things first.

Despite the fact that Rick could see my aura, and we could read each other's mind, our primal drives didn't match in frequency.

To be sure, when a person matches the characteristics we're looking for, our chemistry will respond appropriately at first. We fall in love and it feels like this is the best match. When the keys fit the lock, including our subconsciously held beliefs, we will feel like we have found *The One*. And that was exactly what had happened.

Only years later during a seminar with Dr. Vernon Woolf, who became my mentor, did I discover how the disappointments in my early teenage years had profoundly affected me. The vows that I had taken upon returning from my disillusioned Israel trip had firmed up a belief that being too sexual was not good for me. So I had met my perfect match in Rick. Luckily the judgment hadn't turned off my sexual drive.

As disappointing as it was, retrospectively I am very grateful to Rick. He helped me find the most stimulating spiritual books which became the cornerstones of my spiritual evolution in my life. One book was **The Autobiography of a Yogi** and the other one is called **The Lazy Man's Guide to Enlightenment.**

Naturally, after we got married, I wanted to meditate with him and find our soul union. But try as I might, he did not wish to merge his soul with mine. So the little secret I let you in on here was the fact that I was actually the cause of my own values and beliefs that attracted me to him.

Finally, after plenty of agony, crying myself to sleep, and not getting my needs met, I decided to go out and fulfill at least my meditation needs.

I still remember the moment I dialed the number of a meditation center that had come recommended from a friend. An angelic voice that seared itself into the memory of my soul spoke the following words, "Travel with me the high road to God!" The man's voice who spoke those words, took me straight to the heavens right then and there.

It was a blisteringly cold January night when I made my way to the meditation center in Baltimore for the first time. I was 21 and a half years old and a poor philosophy student, just like I had dreamed of when I was young; I had followed my dreams. When I entered the door of the center, a young man only a few years older than myself greeted me with a handshake. I gazed into his blue glistening eyes and was pleasantly surprised. Don started by guiding our little group into meditation and I rose into sublime light. I noticed that I could meet him in higher states of consciousness and wondered if he had noticed as well.

Whenever I looked at him with my eyes open, I saw a white star blinking, right over his head in the ether. In case this reminds you a little bit of the words from my children's book **Alin Learns to Use His Imagination**, well, true, there is a bit of a biography in my children's book.

Don and I kept encountering each other at this invisible level of reality during the weeks to follow in the weekly training sessions. I knew in my heart of hearts after our third meeting that he was my soulmate. But since he and I were both married, I kept this feeling to myself.

After one month I finally told Don about the woes of my marriage and my lackluster love-life, the physical and spiritual lack I experienced with my husband, and asked Don for techniques that could help me turn my marriage around.

Don definitely was my teacher and knew the right answer. In his wisdom that seemed much greater than mine, he told me that the universe is absolutely listening, and that if I would just take 5 or 10 minutes a day to envision exactly what I wanted to experience in my relationship, and created the feeling that I wished to have and thereby energize the fulfilled feeling in my body, I would soon see changes in my outer life. By holding the blueprint within my own consciousness and within my feeling body, sooner or later he promised I would encounter my dream come true.

In full rapture I listened to Don as he matter-of-factly explained the laws of the universe.

"And there is just one additional secret I need to share with you," Don added, "Be sure not to imagine the face that you believe will bring you this fulfillment. That is the job of the universe!" he emphasized.

"Remember not to manipulate anybody into a particular behavior with the power of your focused mind," he added.

I wondered if he had noticed my adoration of him and wanted to make sure I didn't put him in the picture.

But he was right. I shouldn't put anybody's face in to my desired outcome. Not even my husband at the time. If I were to imagine the face of Rick to be part of my fulfillment, I would squeeze him into a performance which he may not want to participate in. By imagining what I really wanted, which was being in a fulfilling relationship, one in which I was spiritually, creatively and sexually met, I set up a resonant blueprint within myself, independent of any one person or any list. The end result is what counts. The universe then has the opportunity to fill the blueprint that I really wanted.

Just like Don instructed me, I bathed in the sensation of fulfillment for a little while every day in my silent meditation. I imagined being with the right partner and

51

felt the fulfilled feelings which I would have if I had that kind of relationship. I made sure to include the feeling of my spiritual and sexual fulfillment and most of all I was careful *not to imagine a particular face that would bring me this fulfillment.*

I soon got news that my mother was sick and I decided to go back to Germany to be near her. I'm so glad that I did. At least I was able to visit her many times during that last year of her life.

I missed seeing Don, but it was most likely for the better. After all, we were both married.

Eight months later, Don wrote me a handwritten letter to tell me that his wife had started an affair with one of his best friends, and that she had moved out. Don asked me in this letter to come and visit with him in Boulder, Colorado.

I bought my ticket as soon as I could after Rick relented. But alas, despite the immensity of joy that Don and I experienced during the two weeks we stayed together, we both got the same message during our individual meditations on the same day:

We needed to go back to our marriage partners, to finish off our karma. It didn't help that my mother told me that dropping a marriage shouldn't be done like changing socks. Don and I broke off our relationship and returned back to our partners.

Not knowing if my love and attraction for Don that still persisted were totally true, I surrendered my personal will and desire to the divine will, over and over again. I didn't want to be holding on to a desire. Instead I wanted to let go and let God create the perfect expression.

Soon after, Rick and I moved to Boulder and started training in body work, breath work and body centered psychotherapy. I lived with Rick in Boulder while Don lived in the mountains with his wife.

And then a miracle happened. Don's wife got pregnant by yet another man. Instead of acting maliciously, Don simply saw this mishap as a perfect orchestration of the universe. Finally Don and I got the green light to get together. And I'm happy to report we have been together since that time, almost 24 hours a day, 7 days a week, and we kiss the ground we each walk on.

We are working together to express our life's mission, which is to spread the word about how consciousness interacts with matter and how to find the way back home.

At age 17 I had attracted the perfect image of what I thought an attractive man would be like, the man who looked like *The Rifleman*. By choosing *The Rifleman from Santa Fe*, I definitely fulfilled a dream of mine, a desire which had come about through watching a weekly TV show at my grandparents' home. Unwittingly within my own mind and heart I had created a blueprint for a desirable man simply by watching this show.

Furthermore I since had formed judgments in regards to my sexuality at age 16, the universe did its job to find my perfect match: a man who equally didn't wish to have so much sex. The universe was indeed listening and had fulfilled my dreams.

How many times have you forged an image of what you want, just to find that it was not all that you had planned and hoped for? We rarely know our unconscious beliefs, values and judgment, or recall our pains which altered our course. All these will manifest as well unless we do some housecleaning. Moving ahead on the journey to create your Heaven on Earth, soulmate and fulfillment, you will need to also take a look at your unconscious patterns and beliefs.

By imagining the fulfilled feeling of being in a fully satisfying relationship and by not putting a face to my wish, I had allowed the universe to bring the matching soulmate into my life. And this is probably equally important: I had come to a place in my life where I was willing to ask for what I wanted and not judge my needs and desires as negative. I was finally willing to stand up for my own sexual needs, my spiritual needs, and consider them perfectly healthy.

When you wish to create something, you need to hold the blueprints of your dream in your heart and mind. Be sure you imagine and feel the end result you wish to experience. For the moment don't think about the way to get there.

The universe busies itself to fill in all the details. Instead of focusing the details of how we might reach our goal, we best assist the universe by imagining and feeling the final state of happiness, which we will reach in the end.

On your way to your goal, you will be nudged by the universe to take a turn here, to do this, or that. Learning to quiet your mind, to such a degree that you can listen to the inner guidance is of paramount importance. You will be shown which steps to take and directions will come from the inside, from your intuition, instead of coming from the logical and linear mind.

It's an odd thing to realize that a higher dimensional perspective is walking with you, by your side. We might call this energy our guides, or our super soul. Some call it God. Let me just call it "The Universe."

It has a much larger overview than we have and naturally can arrange things to fall into place from a much grander perspective. We only see ourselves living here as the result of actions at a higher dimensional plane. It is as if we see the ripples from the pebbles that have been tossed into a pond. Usually we can't quite see the person who threw the stone. We just see the ripples. But there is a causative energy at a higher dimension. The higher you rise in your soul's perspective, the more you will be one with that causative force, the universe.

There is much turbulent information in the world regarding how to find your soulmate. We all know instinctually that there are souls out there that are a perfect match. If you have a longing for such a partner, it is already a sure sign that the fulfillment is possible. Our desires are the roadmap to our future and to our evolution.

But before we can be happy in a relationship we have to stand on our two feet, emotionally, mentally, and spiritually. Only that way will two equally empowered beings be able to create a greater whole.

Let me tell you about the holy triangle, the sacred design for a fulfilling relationship.

THE ART OF

UNION OF SOULS

Love is what we experience when two (or more) souls merge into One.
This union is experienced as bliss, as love and ecstasy.
No two things can ever occupy the same space at the same time in the
realms of time-space.
However at the level of the soul and beyond,
where we exist beyond time and space, we can merge into union.
Union, merging into oneness, is experienced as love.
Ilona Selke

Union is the drive to experience the state of Oneness,
which is experienced as a feeling of love.
Ilona Selke

Have you ever experienced being in love? Or have you ever felt the feeling of tremendous love for someone or something? What makes us feel so wonderful? Poetically said, we have a feeling of floating or of walking on cloud nine. We see all the similarities, and it is as if we *don't know where one ends and the other one begins.*

This feeling of love often goes hand in hand with losing our sense of being separate. In this state of being intertwined, we feel union with something or someone else, which in turn creates a feeling of being connected at a level that is greater than ourselves.

Sometimes we taste that state of oneness, or that state of being, in a greater field together, sometimes even the feeling that we unite somewhere in the cosmos while making love.

At other times we might feel like we explode and birth into a star together when we make love or when we gaze into each other's eyes.

We might also simply float into the larger universe, not when making love but while being in nature together, or even alone. Other times we find ourselves daydreaming together, gently merging with another being, like our inner guide.

We normally experience a state of ecstasy when falling in love, and desire to absorb everything about the other person into ourselves and to be absorbed by them.

Or we experience this vastness, this exaltation, for example, while giving or watching a birth, or conversely when assisting someone in the process of dying.

Magically, when we are being lifted into other dimensions, it allows us to feel greater and grander than usual. We are lifted into a place, a space or a state which is beyond our own regular sense of selfhood.

Our heart and soul gains wings during such moments and we ascend into the kingdom of love and ecstasy. We somehow are lifted out of our three dimensional sense of self, our normal sense of ego, beyond the ordinary sense of our normal boundaries of self, into a realm where we are more akin to energy.

Quantum science has a name for it: *Wave function.* We often think that matter is made up of particles. However, conventional science is still trying to find the smallest particle that makes up the basic building blocks of matter. Atoms were once thought to be the smallest particle. Atoms were imagined to look much like a billiard ball. But with the advent of *quantum physics* this billiard ball model of life has permanently changed. Physicists had to accept that the deeper they peek into reality, the more slippery its shores become. They now realize that the deeper they stare down the looking glass, the more life looks like the fabric of time-space is made out of waves. At least at the micro-level scientists agree – and this is important to understand for our holy triangle question – namely that the fabric of time-space no longer acts like a mass of particles, but instead acts more like a sea of waves.

Think about it, doesn't making love or loving someone, often create waves of feelings or a flow of energy around you and through you? What is it then that flows through us? Or what is it that flows out of us?

Somehow when we are in love, we experience a greater field of awareness and waves of energies flood us. At times we even feel like we *are inside* the other one, not just physically but also energetically. That is why we love to be in love. *We love the feeling of transcending the ordinary boundaries of our day-to-day ego.*

The good news is that we can learn to enter this state of wave-like-consciousness at will.

We can learn to place our attention from our particle awareness into wave function awareness and thereby enter into a state, at will, of being in love whenever we wish to.

In a nutshell, the secret of the holy triangle is created by merging two individuals, two souls, into a state of union. That creates a state that is greater than the sum of its parts. Here are a few levels in which we may feel union.

There is the obvious level, the physical level of merging. Making love, living together, sharing a house, food, and our gene pool are all ways of merging into union. Although this is a very powerful level of union, in the heart of hearts and deep in our soul, we long for something grander and deeper.

Let me take you through a little tour around the levels of reality.

We all know that we are not just flesh and bones. We are more than just a mixture of atoms. And quantum physics now seems to agree. At a micro-cosmic level, things do not behave like billiard balls, or solid objects. You have probably heard about the EPR experiment (in my previous books I described it, or you can google it). There you will read about the fact that light, where photons were thought to behave like particles, can actually act like waves as well as particles.

To make matters spookier, the way in which way the photons act and respond, depends on who is observing the experiment, depending on what they are looking for.

So, atoms and photons are no longer just billiard balls but also act as waves. Just in terms of making love or loving someone, that makes sense. After all, we feel waves of energy flowing through us when we are in touch with a beloved.

However beyond the levels of form and energy, the sages of old teach us that we exist in a non-dual state of awareness, where we are pure consciousness. Here we can truly enter into states of total union.

Remember that according to the laws of physics, no two things can actually occupy the same space at the same time. In order to experience true oneness, you need to transcend form and even transcend energy (the realm of waves) to enter into a realm of pure consciousness where there is no separation, as we know it, in the realms of time and space.

At each stage of raising our vibration from particle awareness, wave awareness and then to levels beyond duality by entering into pure consciousness, we increasingly experience greater states of love, compassion and understanding.

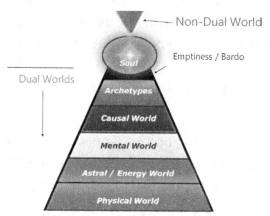

So our quest to find a soulmate and become blissfully happy in union is actually our innate drive to increase our vibrational levels in such a way that our home base is situated in the non-dual realms.

It is here that we can truly experience the merging of two into one. The universe beckons us into ever greater vistas of union, which reveals itself by the desire for union and the wish to transcend the separation.

As we increase our ability to enter heightened states of consciousness, which allows us to experience energy and pure consciousness, our ability to love and to have compassion also increases.

The good news is, that this ascension into union can be learned and practiced at will, given we practice and give ourselves time and patience.

All the steps I describe in this book will guide you to becoming a multidimensional being, to become an energy-based, consciousness-based being. Learning how to manifest effectively is part and parcel of coming to know who you truly are.

Learning how to manifest your soulmate, or anything else in life, becomes easier and more effective when you learn to master your states of consciousness.

Moving from particle-based living to a wave-based, consciousness-based living, forms the basis for being able to create more effectively. One can manifest power-fully and live a life filled with love and bliss. It becomes a life of greater mastery.

Let me draw a little sketch for you to describe how this all applies to the Holy Triangle of Soul Union.

Imagine a person walking in the streets. If he identifies with being a body, the power of this outreach will be as large as his hands can reach. We can touch, fight and support, but only as far as the physical body, or its extension tools, allow us.

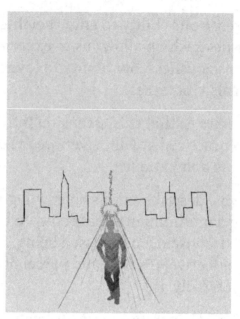

If a person becomes more adept at becoming an energy being, he or she can start affecting energies and matter from a distance. We know this from magical stories of Kung Fu teachers, who have trained to harness the power of their mental and energy body.

If you now imagine this person becoming fully identified with the center of creation, with God, perhaps then you can imagine that his or her capacity can stretch into infinity. He or she sees and encompasses the past and the future. They can have a measurable effect on reality, one that surpasses the person who identifies with the body, and even surpasses the person who identifies with being an energy being.

In the Bible, Jesus said that he and the Father were one. At such a lofty level of union – of the small self with the one large self, i.e. God – the capacity of the small self becomes elevated to the expression of the large One.

Now let us get back to the image of the triangle. Imagine two people sitting opposite each other. As they sit together and focus not onto each other but onto an apex point above themselves, **they are focusing on the meeting point of their souls, which is now forming the apex of the triangle.**

The meeting point of their souls, their mutual apex becomes the space of union and it is here where we transcend separateness. Meeting in this apex is often described as entering true love, or as coming home, or as a state beyond description, a godlike state.

In a nutshell, the secret of the holy triangle is created

by the merging of two individuals into a state of union, a state that is greater than the sum of its parts.

Don and I meet in this apex whenever we can. We create a holy triangle as often as we are conscious enough to do so throughout the day.

If I were to draw a picture I would draw it like this:

We each represent the bottom two corners of the triangle, forming the base of the triangle.

We then extend our imaginary energy lines out of our heads, out into the heavens.

Here we merge our two souls into ONE singularity, into a single unit of consciousness.

I call this our Soul Star, where we feel amazing bliss and love filling our hearts and soul.

In this singular state of consciousness, our souls can meet and we can merge into oneness.

This Holy Trinity is the sacred design of a fulfilling relationship. Instead of focusing just on each other and making the other person responsible for our fulfillment, we reach up into a third space, a meeting place in which we transcend ordinary time and space and meet in the place which RUMI calls, the field.

It allows a third force which is greater than ourselves and greater than our egos, to help govern and guide us. This allows us to become truly unified, which is the ultimate hope, wish and goal for any love.

Out of that unification arises something new. We become the cauldron of Genesis, the cauldron of creation. This unity becomes a fertile field in which stars are born. Don and I did not want to have children, but our work has certainly birthed a lot of stars.

One of our creations is the *Shambala Oceanside Retreat Center* on the North shore of Bali.

In the next chapter, I want to share with you how this simple movement of spiritual awareness into unity has helped me to experience the best sex ever.

OUT OF BODY SEX

Yesterday, my ex-husband came to visit us on our beautiful island in the Pacific Northwest and I asked the following question.

"Tell me," I said with a smile, "What was the most memorable sexual experience you had with me?"

I knew it was a very loaded question, but as you will read further on in this chapter, this question is part of my research for my book which I'm working on by the title **Let's Talk About It – Sexuality Past the Age of Menopause.**

He wasn't surprised, and pondered the question for a moment and then came out with the most surprising answer:

"Oddly enough," he said, "it wasn't actually anything overtly sexual, it was the time when we were still just petting." He went on to describe the time, the place and the location. It had seared itself into his memory. What we can learn from this is it is not the actual sexual interaction that matters, but rather the intensity with which we feel our interaction. The sizzle is what matters.

As I had written earlier, his and my sex life didn't go the way I needed it to go. Against the deepest ethical decisions within my own heart, he suggested that I go and find some other outlets. In other words, he wanted me to find some other lovers to make up for the lack of the sexual love that he was not able to provide.

Gypsies who had read my palm when I was younger,

had foretold that this would happen in my life, and as you know from my book **Dolphins, Love & Destiny** I was not privy to a regular married life as mainstream and Hollywood movies would have it.

The gypsies had told me that I would always have a number of men in my life. This was later confirmed by one of the top psychics, Patty Conklin, a medical intuitive, who works with doctors all across America when regular science has failed them. She told me that if I didn't allow my non-monogamous nature to come out, I would create some kind of disease and leave the planet. Faced with those choices, you can imagine what Don and I chose.

With the story I'm about to tell you, you will see that I was actually very blessed.

When I was sixteen I had already discovered much about sexuality and had had my share of pain and disappointment. I had been lucky enough to have a French lover, who taught me the many secrets of stopping at the right time to heighten the sensation of ecstasy. The greatest secret he taught me was to stop a man just in time before he went over the edge. This means a woman needs to be able to feel where the man is at in his excitement level. Her senses have to be on full alert. She has to know when he is about to explode into ecstasy. And then she has to stop him, or the action, whatever it takes. Hopefully the man equally can give this kind of sensitivity to his partner as well.

The kind of acute awareness that this innocent act requires was actually my first spiritual somatic training. It requested that I was fully present within the bodily and energetic experiences within myself and that of my partner. How else are you going to know when your partner is about to orgasm, and stop just seconds before it?

When I was 18, I had started reading books about discovering the heightened possibilities of sexuality. One book that I kept by my bedside was titled **_Transcendental Sex_** by Jerry Gillies.

Beautiful images sketched in pencil accompanied the description of exercises on how to share the flow of energy between two people instead of focusing on sexual positions and tricky methods of arousal.

The book focused on practicing exercises to slow down enough in order to feel more. This kind of lovemaking filled my heart and stayed with me as an inner compass. When my ex-husband sent me out into the world to find a lover, the universe easily collaborated.

While working as a flight attendant on a flight to Rio de Janeiro, at a time when computers were not what they are today, I was given the task to find the one and only vegetarian passenger on the flight. Apparently he had moved to a new seat, and nobody knew where he had gone to.

I walked through the aisles of hundreds of passengers, and finally stood in front of the one passenger that I thought was the vegetarian one. When I called him by his name he was startled. How did I know his name out of hundreds of people when he changed his seat? He was a classical musician on tour with his entire troop, and it was one of those moments when you look at somebody's eyes and you know that you know them. You know their soul, and you know you will see them again.

Many people take this to mean that they're soulmates. And maybe you can say that it is a sort of soulmate. The ancient Greeks believed that the soulmate was one unit that was split into two halves, the masculine and feminine half. Later on these two split halves would try to find each other again.

The only problem of course is that such metaphors confuse people. Ultimately we incarnate through many lifetimes as a male or female. At times we are more female as a male and sometimes more male as a female. We walk through all these nuances to discover the integration of the male and female principles within ourselves.

Expecting to find the other fitting half, which is split off from ourselves and to expect that to be our soulmate is sort of an outdated metaphorical model from antiquity.

But by and large most people feel that a soulmate is someone that when you look into their eyes, there is something that is deeply moved within yourself. You connect at a level beyond the visible realm. You connect at a deep soul level.

As you can imagine, we have lots and lots of those type of encounters waiting for us once we are able to enter the level of soul awareness. Finding a soulmate means that we have to be able to reach into the levels of soul awareness ourselves. It also means that quite a number of souls could match that description. Would we want to marry all of them? Probably not!

As we evolve into greater and greater abilities to reach

a higher state of awareness, into soul realized levels and beyond, we will meet and merge and melt our soul awareness with many others. Ultimately, God is said to be the entirety of everything, and everyone. It would therefore stand to reason that we are soulmates with every single soul imbued being.

Let's fast-forward. This amazing classical musician and genius introduced me to the worlds of art, music and a depth of connection that I had not yet experienced.

With the blessings of my ex-husband, we decided to go on a little vacation together and took a bicycle tour along the Rhine River in Germany. Let us call him Al. He was not quite twice my age, but past his mid-thirties and I was twenty.

It was late afternoon of the first day of our three day tour, when we decided to take a detour through the forest to find a little inn for the night.

We had both been biking in slow motion, barely pedaling enough to stay on our bikes. Floating through the late afternoon sun, I savored the light as it was filtering through the trees, and deeply breathed in the musty smell of the forest floor. The slowness, the misty sunlight and sharing this almost motionless stillness with another being produced an incredible atmosphere between us. It is true that when you slow down, your senses heighten and that is when the magic begins.

As we stopped to look at a room for the night at the inn, the air between us was filled with a supernatural presence and I felt such amazing connectedness without any words. I detected a little questionable look in the innkeeper's eyes when he ushered us into a room. Remember that this was around 1981. Maybe he wanted to make sure nothing strange was going on between such a young woman and this older man and we were given a room with two separate beds which were positioned head to head.

My first best sex ever happened actually without getting naked.

We settled in as darkness fell late this summer night, as it does in the Northern European hemisphere. Both of us were still mesmerized by the charge that hung in the air from our slow-motion afternoon. The universe had magically arranged our beds to be head-to-head instead of side-by-side. We took this opportunity to discover union in a totally new way.

Twilight was settling in and the subtle shades of our bodies melted into the darkness of the night. Slowly we started reaching out overhead, searching for our hands to meet. As we started discovering first our fingers and then our hands, we started moving our hands in unison – just as slowly as we had been bicycling that day.

As if in a dance, we moved our hands and arms and started to explore and discover each other. At moments the dance of our hands was slower, so light as to barely touch. At other moments our hands were more passionately intertwined, until we let our breath crescendo, savoring the intensity of each other, followed by deeper breath that helped us to slow down again.

Engulfed in this dance of our breath, touch and the silent spaces in between, I started feeling like I was floating. I could feel Al not only with my hands and arms, but I could also feel and see him in the ethers, as if we were dancing above our heads. We tumbled and rose in our inner worlds with just the hint of a touch of our bodies. We rolled into a subtler dimension and flew higher than we had ever gone before. We no longer needed our bodies to touch each other. Our breath intensified, slowed, deepened, and we touched each other to the core in this cosmic union.

Colors swirled through my mind and we made love with our hands while we made love out of our bodies. Unifying our astral bodies, we were feeling more alive than ever, and found ourselves breathless, speechless and fully ecstatic.

We made love without leaving our separate beds. Without getting naked we had experienced a crescendo of union that touched both our souls to the deepest core. To this day it remains one of my most memorable sexual union moments, superseded only by those times in which my lover and I merged our bodies and souls at the same time. As you can imagine I took this art into the love life that awaited me with Don. But at this moment in time, I had not yet met Don.

Merging the seen with the unseen, merging the felt world with the ephemeral world, merging souls into union with God is indeed what most people recall as their most profound and satisfying lovemaking.

The art of merging your heart and soul is an art that you will be able to take with you throughout your life, into the next life. It will certainly remain long past the time when your body is no longer at its prime, and when the body may not function the same way it did when you were in your twenties.

Where attention goes, energy flows. THE UNIVERSE IS LISTENING every second of your day. Whatever you truly hold in your heart, mind and soul, and I might add what is in your subconscious and deeper often unconscious beliefs, is what will manifest.

The moment you declare to the universe what you truly and deeply wish to do, have or be, the universe will move you toward that fulfillment. Sometimes that fulfillment will come instantly, sometimes it will come slowly, requiring you to grow into a new self-image first.

Set up your inner and outer goals. Set out to dream what is possible or even at first what seems impossible. Your dreams and goals will take you on your journey of greater evolution. We grow in stages, so it is good to set goals or wishes in stages as well.

As I mentioned in the research for the book I am still working on, *Let's Talk About It,* I talk about sexuality past the age of menopause. In the questionnaire that I passed out to many people to gather information for the book, I had posed the question: What was the most memorable sex you had? What about it made it memorable?

You might ask yourself the same question now: What was the most memorable love making for you? And that leads to the next question: What kind of sexuality would you like to experience?

We may not ever stop to think about it, but if we wish to grow, to evolve to dream bigger, we do need to also think about how we wish to be, as a sexual being. Money, houses, work, our purpose in life and even our spiritual evolution are all perfect goals to set. But what about your sexuality?

Therefore I would like to ask you: What kind of sexuality would you like to experience? If you were to dream big and really got what you really wanted, what would you wish to experience in this aspect of yourself?

As with all things, we need to create the inner experience in ourselves first. This does three things:

First of all, we clarify what we want and what is important to us. We do need to know where we would like to go in order to arrive at the destination of our choice. Many people leave the aspect of their sexuality up to chance. But in order for the universe to assist us in creating a better life, we need to ask ourselves the question: What do I want?

No answer will ever last for eternity. We grow and evolve. Each step takes us to the next level. From the new vista we will be able to choose new destinations. But if we never set out to climb the first hill or mountain, we may likely never see much more than the valley we are in.

Secondly, we pre-create the internal experience independent of outer experiences. That way we are not dependent on the outer event to fulfill us, but instead we bring the fulfillment that is already within us to the event or experience. We no longer define our happiness by what we get, but by who and what we are.

Thirdly, by feeling the fulfillment in advance, we give the universe the blueprint of what it can then fill with life. This blueprint can best be understood by the universal energy when we feel it in its fulfillment. In the olden days it was said that you had to have a positive thought, then we add the imagery. Now we add feeling.

Over time we collectively discover what the secret ingredients are to powerfully co-create with the universe. Each decade brings with it new insights, new discoveries.

As you read in the last chapter about the Holy Triangle, and the Ascension of Soul awareness, you will understand how the vantage point, or the focal point of our soul increases the power with which we create. We not only get more focused and embrace greater expanses of time and space, start to know the future and the past, but we also gain a more refined ability to co-create with the universe.

More toward the end of the book about this.

Back to the research answers about sexuality past menopause. Some of the answers I received from the questionnaire were staggering to read.

Some of the people's best memories were about making love in nature, under the trees or by the crashing waves of the ocean. Some best memories were steamy, like making love on the hood of the car, by exploring taboos and by letting down their guards.

But by and large the utmost memorable and satisfying experiences of being sexual all had one component in common: A moment of transcendence of self and experiencing true union.

When the boundaries of the two individuals disappear and vanish into union, when the two become one, and merge with the cosmos, that stays as the most memorable experience in people's minds.

In the heart of hearts, many men and women do yearn and hope for a deep sense of union. A union of soul and a union of bodies.

However, it appears that for most people, the different aspects of union: being sexual, being in love, and being connected to God, are located in three different worlds, if not universes altogether. Sex, love and soul union appear to occupy three totally different parts of our brain as Helen Fisher describes it so eloquently in her book **_Why We Love._**

How do we unify these three aspects of love? Our bodily chemistry, our love and feelings, as well as our soul's desire for union?

Many women miss the soulfulness in their male partners, and secretively hope that they will find their soulmate, who will automatically know all her unspoken wishes and that he responds telepathically to every twist and turn of her often unruly heart and mind.

However, it is up to us to become the "soul aware" person first, with us having the ability to see deeply into the soul of another that qualifies us to become and find a true soulmate.

Magically, love pulls us beyond our normal confines and boundaries of our ego. Love offers us a portal into an infinitely greater experience than just being our individual selves.

Yet another equally important question is: What do we do once we've found a soul love, a soulmate and get married? How do we make that love last?

HOW TO MAKE LOVE LAST

UNTIL OLD AGE

Let's fast-forward our movie about 35 years down the road. By now, I am 56 years old and Don is 62. Don and I have been married and together for 34 years, pretty much together 24 hours a day.

We are truly in love and in a soul-union relationship beyond my wildest hopes and dreams. To this day, we still kiss the ground the other walks on every day.

Both of us are definitely past menopause by now, although we feel like we are in our twenties. Having led a vegetarian life without any alcohol, without smoking, drugs, or TV for that matter and keeping up with our daily yoga, our daily meditations (as best as we can), and drinking our green juices daily, has definitely worked in our favor.

Last week we led our last dolphin swim seminar in Florida, which we had been doing for 25 years. Don taught the first seminar with me and then had to leave, while I taught the second seminar.

During the seminar, we swam with wild dolphins half the day and spent an additional two hours per day together as a group doing inner work.

On the first day I took the participants through a guid-ed imagery exercise where they saw themselves through the eyes of a dolphin. Slipping into the mind of a dol-phin, swimming side-by-side next to themselves, I asked the participants to look at their own energy body and notice the areas in their human aura which were lit up and which were still dark.

I've lead this particular guided imagery exercise over the last 25 years with people from all walks of life, all ages, and all kinds of nationalities, Western, Asian, and African people alike.

Typically people report back that when they see themselves through the eyes of a dolphin, their upper chakras are more lit up, whereas their lower chakras are usually darker, less lit and less alive. Interestingly enough, merging with the dolphin's mind yields similar results. The results are very different from participants seeing themselves through the eyes of any other being. The dolphins, without fail, encourage humans to ignite their lower chakras, become more playful, more expressive of their sensual energies, and become more alive in these parts of their body.

Some people see darkness around their heart area, which needs to be opened up more, but by and large the dolphins encourage us as humans to ignite the lower chakras, and increase our "Joy of Life" or "Joie de vivre."

The second part of this dolphin journey is even more astounding and often breathtaking.

I invite people to choose someone to experience the ultimate union of soul with. I tell them to either pick a dolphin, angel, or someone human that they wish to merge with in their soul.

Next, I ask the participants to imagine that they have a soul star above their head, and to coalesce into this single point of their soul diamond. While each person does so, I also ask them to imagine that their counterpart is doing the same thing at the same time.

Soul star to soul star, diamond to diamond, both beings begin to look at each other from this super heightened dimension of pure consciousness.

The seat of the soul is a realm beyond time and space and although it is hard to describe, we know it when we are entering it. At this level we don't really use our eyes and we don't really feel like we still have a body. We simply enter this primal state of pure pristine awareness which can be felt like a pinnacle of bundled consciousness above or beyond our crown chakra. The soul star is not actually located outside of our body. It is, in fact, located beyond any dimension as we know it. We don't float out and we don't go anywhere, but our minds do use these metaphors of distance and movement to make sense of spacelessness and timelessness.

Each of us is connected to the core of the universe, to all that is, to the center of creation, to God. We can imagine it as a line that connects us to the core of God or the core of the universe. However, these are metaphors our mind uses to make sense of our perceptions of reality. These perceptions are so far beyond what our human mind is used to thinking of that we are somewhat limited by our human imagination.

It is important to note here, and one of the most important sentences that I read in the book *The Lazy Man's Guide To Enlightenment*: We are made of the one and only stuff there is, and it pulsates in us day in and day out. There is no higher and lower, no good or evil at our core. We are all of the same stuff.

As the participants rise along their imaginary light-line to the center of creation, they of course find that the other being, the dolphin or their soulmate, is also rising with them. As they do, they both start to spiral around each other's soul diamond. They spiral together, higher and higher in their own ascension to the very same center of creation.

I ask everyone to ascend deeper and deeper, or higher and higher into the center of creation, to the degree that each one is willing to experience total union. Mostly everyone, in all the decades I have taught this form of union, has gone to these incredible heights or depths until the two soul diamonds merge into singularity, into one single point of is-ness, into the ONE.

Union is felt as love. We feel love as we are able to interpenetrate and share the same space with one other.

This unification, where two (or more) become one, is indeed always felt as love.

God is said to be love. God is the ultimate home, where supreme union of "all that is" happens. It is the point of singularity of "all that is."

In the process of coalescing everything into this oneness, we experience the sensation of love. Love is the superseding unity of two or more.

If you learn to intentionally merge your soul diamond, the seat of your soul, into oneness with your beloved, you will experience the most profound sense of bliss, profound ecstasy and love that you can imagine.

Unfailingly, 80% or more of all the people with whom I

do this guided imagery exercise, whether I do it in large audiences of 1000 people or in small groups, intuitively know how to merge their soul star into union with God.

Union is embedded and woven into the very structure of the universe. Everything strives to merge, to enter into oneness, even if for just a brief moment. Out of this merging emerges a new being. This is the cauldron of true genesis. Love is the feeling we get at the moment of the most profound union. Love is the force that glues everything together. We at once lose all sense of self and we are liberated as we fly into the greatest all-ness that is, and at the same time we become one. Oneness is where we come from, and it is where we return to.

This union, where two merge into (oneness) singularity, brings us such profound understanding of what it means to be "all that is."

By now, I believe that the path of union is indeed the shortest and fastest way to heightened states of consciousness. It is the fastest path to Self- and God-realization.

Whether you merge the singularity of your individual self with the oneness in a solo journey, or whether you go into union with an (imaginary) deity like the Tibetans do, or if you do this with your eyes open while gazing into the depth of the soul of your beloved, these paths all lead into the great union and deliver us into bliss and into the One.

This will allow you to make love until old age. Let me show you how.

As I mentioned earlier, Don and I had led our last dolphins swim seminar together and he had had to leave after the first group. We had spent the last 10 days and nights apart and we were eager to spend precious time together, in bed as well as out in nature.

We usually spend twenty-four hours per day together. Don reads my every thought and feeling, as I do his. Our mutual and primary values in life were soul realization and God realization even before we met. Needless to say, we were very harmonious, albeit very different in our styles.

Besides focusing on our soul's light, we also had practiced the art of manifesting and co-creating increasingly beautiful realities together throughout all these years.

However much I had missed Don, as we laid in each other's arms the first morning, I was keenly aware of a subtle anxiety in myself. The previous night I had had an unsettling dream in which Don had a love affair with an alien female. She was not very humanoid and looked more like the opera singer from the movie *The Fifth Element*.

Interestingly enough, I hadn't been even the slightest bit jealous in my dream, nor worried. It felt as though Don had to learn a particular lesson from this alien female.

However, this wise understanding vanished somewhat upon waking and my human emotions awoke. I was unsettled by the meaning of the dream.

We started to cuddle in a deep, love filled, embrace. When my gaze met Don's blue eyes, he showered me with an overflowing abundance of love. But my heart wasn't there yet. The dream still had me in its grips.

What was I to do? Play along? Disturb such a beautiful moment? But what was it inside of me that was not on the same page with him this very moment? I was a bit disturbed.

In moments of wavering, I recall that honesty is my primary principle. It stands like a pillar in such moments of doubt or wavering and gives me the backbone and stability. Despite the discomfort it might create, I decided to share my inner states, and also my dream.

I shared my worries which arose after the dream and that I was wondering if we were still meant to be together. I questioned myself and wondered why I had dreamed up this scenario.

This may seem a bit over the top for most people. But I can assure you, as you will see, attending to the little details brings great rewards.

Instead of shirking from the questions, we both took the time to feel the feelings, and to stay present with the doubts and fears.

In this safe cocoon, Don and I started ascending into the presence of our soul. We had trained ourselves to feel the star diamond of each other's soul. I call it the soul diamond, or soul star. Beyond that, we meet in our combined soul star, which is the one point we share together. It is our stable ground, located beyond the turmoil of humanness. This is where we can consciously touch into God, into oneness and be in divine love.

Each and every one of us has such a soul star. Most of the time people are not trained to notice the core of their consciousness with any amount of clarity. Rarely do they stay still enough to merge their individual soul star or diamond consciously into union and to observe what happens when they do.

In all honesty, to become aware of this takes practice and time. But as I told you in the above experiment where the seminar participants merged into union with a dolphin, more than 80% of the people had the most profound experience of oneness. All of us have this ancient wisdom and ability deeply embedded within.

As Don and I were lying in bed, I felt calmer having found our rock solid soul connection and I got in touch with deeper layers of my emotions.

Instead of being impatient with me, or wishing that I was already happy, Don took the time to gently listen not only with his ears, but extended his tentacles of his feeling body. Beyond that, he extended the subtle antennae of his soul in order to meet me at the most sublime and refined realms of consciousness.

When I noticed that Don was actually reaching deeply into me, I felt like I was being touched, held and cradled in the most profound way possible.

From within the greatest depth of my emotional self, maybe even a primordial sense of self, a profoundly sensitive and vulnerable essence, I was safely received. Don and I love to call this *"The Pink"*. I started ascending through the higher octaves of consciousness bringing with me the many layers of my emotions, my body and energy.

Higher and higher we rose, keeping up with each other. We had practiced staying aware of not only our own presence but we had also trained to stay aware of each other during this ascension process. I let my breath flow through me fully, up and out and then, in my imagination, allowed this breath to circle into Don. This ensured that my consciousness stayed connected to my body and my feelings.

Our perception and sharing refined itself ever more in this spiraling dance of ascension back to the source. Space became meaning, and our spiraling dance had become a cauldron of genesis.

Impossible to describe in words, ecstasy took over. We held each other in a tight physical embrace, while cherishing the ascension of our soul's awareness, entering into ever higher octaves of union. Waves upon waves of ecstasy and gratitude flooded through my heart and body and I expanded in my love and my ability to open to Don. Foremost, I opened more deeply to the sublime union of our souls into God.

Don, God, oneness, love, being the entire universe and the profundity of this form of lovemaking is beyond what we can understand with our normal minds. In a way, it takes one to know one, and in order to fully understand we have to experience it ourselves.

But in the heart of hearts we all know that this state exists. In the depth of our soul we know this kind of merging is possible. Most of us yearn for it. Whether you are reading this for the first time, or you have already experienced it for yourself, you most likely know it's possible.

When Don and I returned from this peak of ecstasy to normal states of consciousness, we both felt like we had made love in the profoundest of ways. My heart had totally melted, all fears had subsided and I was open to love and to union with Don here on this earth more than ever before.

The next day Don and I made love including our bodies, slowing down often enough to notice the nuances of what we were feeling. It is important to slow down in order to bring our awareness into our body and connect our energy wave into the subtle dimensions. When we make love in the body, we will be rewarded grandly by raising our awareness to heaven.

As we orgasmed closely at the same time, we consciously catapulted our awareness up into our soul star and beyond, offering our orgasmic bliss state into the hands of God. Floating in this immense expanse of our lovemaking, our hearts spiraled upward through our crown into the cosmic state of union, the union we truly yearn for.

This type of lovemaking, whether it takes on the sexual physical component which we normally associate with lovemaking, or not, will fulfill us until the day we transcend into another dimension.

Love arises when we leave the sense of separation and enter any kind of union. This can be experienced as a small form of growing beyond ourselves or as a mind blowing state of ecstasy.

Soul-love is available to all of us independent of our age, status, or our sex. This soul love can be experienced with all things and all beings and will become our norm as we ascend in our evolution.

Let me tell you how a woman used the process of the *Living From Vision*® course to create the love of her life.

MANIFESTING MADE EASY

Lounging in her bed in her house at our *Shambala Oceanside Retreat* center in Bali, Jocelyne had opened the glass doors and the ocean was almost touching her feet. The wind gently wafted the fuchsia colored curtains into her room and we sat on her bed to talk.

She was at a pivotal point in her life. As a beautiful, vibrant and young looking sixty year old woman, she was searching to manifest the next level of meaning for the next stage of her life. She had hopes and dreams and was ready to add another exciting phase to her life. In this phase she wanted to find her soulmate and express more of her life's purpose. But she wasn't sure how this was going to come about.

Jocelyne was staying with us at our *Shambala Oceanside Retreat* center in Bali, Indonesia as she was teaching a group of women on how to find their joy in life.

As you know the adage: *"Knock and the door will be opened."* Or: *"Ask and you shall receive,"* she practically had planted herself right in the middle of *Shambala,* a beautiful place of peace, where she was hoping to find her answer.

I still don't know what started our conversation in this direction, but as it is so often in life, when you are in the flow, the right questions get asked or the right answers just flow out.

As soon as she told me of her dreams, I told her how

the techniques in the *Living From Vision®* course would be able to help teach her to discover the details of her dream and then she would manifest from the inside out, instead of pushing from the outside.

All too often people don't really know what their purpose is. I told Jocelyne that the fourth week segment was fully about discovering more about her purpose for this segment of her life.

Something gave me the hunch that she would be a fabulous coach and teacher. Therefore, I told her that once she mastered these manifestation methods, she could also choose to help countless people to improve their lives here on Earth by teaching the *Living From Vision®* methods.

Many people have heard of the ancient teachings – how thought creates reality. However, the desired results don't happen by just reading a book. *Many people seek to understand the practical steps of how to manifest.* We all need a teacher or a teaching to get us going on the right track, and books alone don't give us the hands on experience we need. We want to become adept at multidimensional living and how to manifest our dreams, and that requires training of a different level of our mind.

Jocelyne set out to study the *Living From Vision®* course once she returned to Canada to create her next steps in her life.

However, as soon as she started the LFV course, she called me up and asked for a coaching session. Her problem: *She could not really visualize anything.* Quite a few people tell me that they can't visualize. Thank God I had the remedy!

To prove to her that she was indeed able to *see* her inner worlds, I did an experiment with her. I love to do this particular experiment with anybody who tells me they can't visualize. Join me now on this little exercise because, who knows, you might be able to help another person gain confidence in their own inner perceptions.

Firstly, you may already know, that some people use their visual perceptions more than other senses. Some people are the visual types. Inwardly and outwardly, they see all the nuances and colors and they make postcards out of every scene they see. They are great decorators or designers and do well with the visual arts. I belong to that category.

Then there are the kinesthetic types, the people who feel more, rather than see. When they enter a room, they feel the energy instead of seeing all the radiant colors, shapes and forms. They typically feel overwhelmed by trying to get perspectives, seeing the forest because of all the trees, as the saying goes. They may feel the vibes in the room, and navigate mostly on feeling rather than seeing.

They have a harder time making timetables, seeing the future before their eyes, and would rather feel their way through life.

Others yet may be highly sensitive to smells in the environment. Others yet are keenly aware of sounds. We all use our senses differently. In truth, we all use a mix of our senses, but generally speaking we have a predominant sense that we use. Jocelyne didn't feel very confident about her ability to see things and was not sure she could do the LFV exercises well enough to succeed.

In my coaching session with her I walked her through a simple exercise that gave her the confidence that she needed. You can do this with me right now.

"Close your eyes, and imagine a tree." I told her.

"Now imagine that on one side of the tree there is a red dog. To the other side of the tree there is a blue dog."

Please try this yourself now and you may be surprised and later help another person to open their understanding of the inner workings of their mind.

"Now take your index finger and point to the red dog." I finished.

Jocelyne pointed to her left, the area where she perceived the red dog.

"Wow, you did it!" I exclaimed. Jocelyne was perplexed. Indeed she had sort of seen where the red dog was located. Despite the fact that she thought she couldn't see anything inside, she surprised herself today. Could it be that easy?

I pointed out to her that somehow in her mind she knew exactly where the red dog was. She was puzzled. Indeed she had *kind of seen* the red dog to the left side of her imaginary tree. She didn't *see* the dog or the tree in brilliant colors, but she kind of saw and knew that the red dog was on the left side of the tree. She sort of saw and knew that the blue dog was on the other side.

From this day onward she had the confidence to "see" inwardly and to use her "imagination", which meant her ability to represent something in an abstract way internally, to navigate to success.

At times people think they have to see perfect images similarly to how they see with their eyes open. That is not the case. We don't have to be able to see crystal clear images in order to manifest effectively. Every person has their own preferred state of how they "see" or simply "know".

It is true that the more we relax, the clearer the images become. I have days where my images are fuzzy and some days my internal images are crystal clear and have many details in them. I have taught seminars for over ten-thousand hours and I've helped people, who had never in their life been able to visualize, suddenly be able to see inwardly.

What is the trick, you may ask?

One important factor is to know that all of us have an internal system of representation.

The other one is to give ourselves time. We need to go slowly enough to drop into lower brainwave states. Some people drop more easily into this dreamy state than others. Others drop quickly, even so deep that they bypass the threshold to visualize into the near sleep state. At this level people are beyond the ability to grasp the images, and they go into the Theta brainwave bordering on the Delta brainwave state.

That is where a person nods off. Men are particularly prone to this. But with practice, we can all learn to keep our attention focused right in the middle, around 7.8 hertz, the Schumann frequency, in order to do imagery work.

In higher meditation levels, you will actually want to get the body into a very deep state of relaxation and yet

91

at the same time you will raise the focus of your attention into a realm where your brain will oscillate at higher brainwave states, instead of lower frequencies. Part of your brain will go into the Gamma brainwave frequency.

It is important to understand that when setting goals and wishing to manifest something, the brain waves states which we enter will be naturally dreamy. This is where we have access to deeper levels of our mind. The level where we are daydreaming is found in the Alpha brainwave frequency. Some people have a hard time calming their mind down enough in order to enter this meditative state. Other people drop so deeply and quickly that they slip into Theta brainwave state and start sleeping.

Brainwave Frequencies

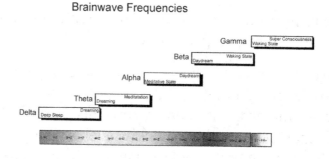

In the *Living From Vision®* daily exercises, which I still use daily, I follow guided suggestions of imagery to prepare my day and energize my goals.

Many people get up and just start with their daily habits such as going to the bathroom, brushing their teeth and starting to boil water.

By doing that, we unconsciously create our day.

Successful and happy people all tell me that the first thing they do upon waking is to start focusing on gratitude, connecting with their inner potential, or their highest expression for the day.

By utilizing our ability to focus, we touch into the higher parts of our mind. By pre-creating our future and setting up a blueprint for success we set the hologram that is in our mind into motion.

Without collecting our attention to a greater vista, we drift like leaves in the wind of our daily demands. Our actions will be the dictates of what is expected of us or what our subconscious programs are creating for us. We will *create*, one way or another.

Jocelyne was loving the daily guided imagery exercises and was starting to feel more and more positive. She noticed that the Refocusing Technique had helped her to become more positive in her focus and even with her words. She had had a habit of focusing on what was not working. Whenever she encountered what she didn't like, she now re-phrased herself and redirected her attention immediately toward what she wanted. In Buddhist teachings, the saying goes that we need to heed our mind, thoughts and speech. Watch how you speak every day. Keep a mental diary of how you use your words and what you focus on. Because whatever you place more of your attention on, is the seed that you water. This does not mean not to deny what is not working. We do need to be able to differentiate and this helps us to determine where we really want to go. Focusing on what you really want means that we simply notice what is not working and then re-focus on what we really want. In that, we water the seeds of our dreams.

Learn to say what you mean and also mean what you say. The more focused your mind becomes, the more quickly your thoughts will manifest.

A few weeks later, during a coaching session, Jocelyne told me that she had met a man who seemed to fit the list of attributes she wanted to have in a partner. But somehow it just didn't zing. All the items on her list matched, but it only felt so-so.

Instead of looking for the items on our list, it is good to go into the end result and the feeling we wish to have. I told Jocelyne to simply imagine and really feel the state of fulfillment that she wanted to experience and to let the universe arrange the rest. Remember, you are the one that gets to be the eyes, ears and hands of the universe. The universe then helps set everything into motion from a much higher perspective. THE UNIVERSE IS LISTENING, but we do have to ask.

Next, Jocelyne went about her life and decided to take the *Living From Vision®* Teacher and Coach training. She taught a number of very successful courses. The student that touched her the most was her ninety-year-old mother. This woman felt like she now had a magic wand in her life and wanted to dream up the next adventures for her life. We can all be lighthouses to our friends and family and then to our world at large. Soon the next vacation time came around again: Six weeks in Bali!

Jocelyne met up with her daughter in Bali, spent precious time with her and a girlfriend and again came to stay at *Shambala*. On her trip to Bali, the magical thing happened! She met a man who was traveling also, and was widowed. Soon Cupid struck and the magic of two souls, both on their path to enlightenment, found a venue for union. Jocelyne had not focused on how she would meet that man of her dreams. Instead she kept feeling the fulfillment that she would feel if she already had what she wanted.

The universe gets the blueprint from what we place our attention on. We can either spin our wheels, or we can pre-envision the goal we wish to reach. The universe arranges all the roads and those that populate our road. Imagine it as if we live in a Multiverse in which we can dial in the kind of end result we wish to have. By the virtue of your focus, you navigate through all the possible alternate, parallel realities.

Since we are currently on our road of life, we might as well set out to have the best life. To some people their goals may be a better home, a car, more income, a better job or to find their life's purpose. To others it might be the wish to merge their soul with a soulmate, or even the One, to be in enlightened union with the All with God.

Whatever your goals are, they are yours. Your wishes are your stepping stones to your next level of expression, expansion and your understanding of the universe on your path of awakening. Each step moves us along, further and further into the mystery of life. We will naturally be drawn to the center of creation and understand all that is, in time.

Did Jocelyne have to "think" about where to meet her soulmate? No! When we connect consciously to a higher tune in our life, the arrangement comes from levels beyond our conscious mind. Just how exacting the universe is, and how impeccable the alignment is, I will share in my next story.

MANIFESTING MONEY OUT OF AIR

When Don and I met, I was 21 years old and he was a chimney sweep. Less than half a year after we met I needed to move back to Germany because my mother was dying. Don was inspired by the ease with which I moved to Germany and it inspired him to finally make a move from the East Coast of the USA to the famous New Age city of Boulder, Colorado. However he needed to move an entire household with his previous wife.

Don had read the book **Master Key System** by Charles F. Haanel, detailing methods and techniques on how to use your mind to create a better life. To turn book knowledge into results, Don took a class in the *Master Key System*, taught by a man by the name of Johnson.

Don calculated that his move would cost him about $6300 USD, money which he didn't have. With the innocence of a beginner, Don decided to give the methods of the *Master Keys* a try in order to magically manifest the funds he needed.

The methods are age-old. There are no real secrets. The real secret lies in having enough belief in a magical universe and the daily application of the methods in order to create results.

Just like it said in the book, Don sat down in silence and imagined that he had the $6,300 USD in his bank account. He practiced this until he had that special feeling in his body and heard the "YES it is so." Don had a very sincere desire and need. In his heart of hearts, he really felt that his wish was not unreasonable, although it was a bit of a stretch to trust that it could come about!

Don imagined and rehearsed a feeling as though his wish had already come about. Daily, he bathed in this fulfilled feeling.

Just about six weeks later, an out of this world miracle happened. Don received an unexpected check in the mail by the tax office. Low and behold, the tax office had sent Don a check for exactly the amount that he had visualized. When he saw the check with his own eyes, he felt the universe wobble! How could this be? The tax office didn't owe him any money, and there was no logical explanation to receiving this check in the mail. Our current western world view teaches us that the world operates according to scientific laws. We believe it. But this check demonstrated to Don that *the universe was indeed listening.*

Don had dared to dream, a big dream, and the universe cooperated. Don got his answer. The fact that such miracles happen should wake us up out of our slumber. Who actually is listening? Is it the universe? Where are its ears? Who is sending that check? Who is arranging such unlikely events? This is spooky!

Don had devised his own laboratory and developed his own set of rules by which he wanted to prove to himself that these laws of consciousness worked!

If the universe is able to listen to our silent thoughts, then we are not living in the kind of universe that science portrays. There is not a hard and cold world out there. We are not the peons in a clockwork universe. But to communicate effectively with the universe, one has to learn a few basics.

By declaring what he wanted, writing it down, asking the universe for support and imagining it already done, he had done some of the most important steps.

What baffles me is that this is not taught in school. We all need to know that we live in a living universe, a Consciousness Interactive Universe. If it works for Jesus and other prophets, rishis and yogis, then it applies, in principle at least, to every single being in the universe.

With the money from the check that arrived in his mailbox, out of the blue from the tax office, a check that was not his tax return, Don was able to move their house and household from Baltimore to Colorado, just like he had imagined.

The surprise came later, when the tax office contacted Don to let him know that they inadvertently had sent him a check that was meant for someone else. The tax office wrote to him at the perfect time. Don had already made the extra funds back in earnings and was able to pay back the tax office as requested. The point to note here is the absolute perfection of timing, of alignment of all events. When Don really needed the money, he had received it. The miracle check came in the mail.

Let me ask you: Who is listening?

Think about it! Really think about it. What does it say about how life works!?

It is not Google or Amazon, with their home devices that are listening into co-create these kind of miracles.

Who is arranging all the miraculous manifestations?

Who makes all of this happen?

Did the yogis we met in India simply know a few more details of how to manifest miracles? If so, what were they!

Simply put, for these more *ordinary* miracles to happen, such as the one that Don had experienced, all he needed to do is provide a blueprint of the perfect outcome. The details are arranged by the universe. We don't need to think of the way to get the destination. We simply need to feel like we have already arrived at our destination.

I wonder how many people marvel about this utterly miraculous fact of life. We live in a Consciousness Interactive Universe!

Why did it work so quickly?

Don had barely read about the methods called the **Master Keys**, and he immediately got results. His subconscious mind had been open to believe in a greater power, due to the stories the author told in the book. These extraordinary stories and theories presented in the *Master Keys* book provided the fuel needed to make Don's visions become reality.

Don's teacher of the *Master Keys* class had given a live example. He wanted to use this method to manifest a houseboat for himself. He only had started discovering the secret workings of the universe after life had dealt him a serious blow. He had lost his house, his business and most of what he had owned, before he turned to study the higher laws of the universe. The loss had become his blessing and, though life had taken such an abysmal turn, he was filled with renewed hope. The blows were as if the universe had given him a push to wake him up. Trying to prove to himself the effectiveness of these tools, Johnson visualized owning a houseboat. Instead of giving up, he reached up.

One day he got a call from his attorney who was helping him with the loss of his business and told him that due to a new tax law he was entitled to a government refund for exactly the amount that the houseboat was going to cost. Even at a time when all hope was gone, when all seemed dire, this man was able to manifest a way to have a house, live in style again and have it paid for. Instead of burying his head in the sand, he stood up to his fate, used his focus and re-imagined his life successfully.

Later, Johnson rebuilt his life, now based on a totally new understanding of life and became a millionaire and successful entrepreneur.

Stories such as this one provide fuel for our minds and hearts to create belief in a higher order or power. Whatever this force is, we can learn to live as beings from a higher order independent of our religious beliefs.

As humans we vicariously learn and we love to imitate one another. That is how we learned to survive, built cultures, and how we ensure the longevity of our species. Stories like these that we share help us create a community and a feeling that it is OK to live miraculously. They set the stage to feel part of a larger group that lives in a Consciousness Interactive Universe. Learning how to focus our consciousness, navigate time-space and how to grow in the light and love of our soul, enhances our human potential.

The stories in this book are from modern day people who have made miracles happen. As you read about other humans doing them, you will find the excitement and understanding growing within you.

If normal mortals like you and me, have created miracles by seeing, believing and feeling the end-result of their dreams in full color inside their minds and hearts, then you can do the same.

The secret laws of the universe are currently not taught in the universities in the western world. We are not taught that our mind interfaces with the reality around us. Sports people are using these methods and discovering what works best and what doesn't work as well. They understand the subtle interplay of our consciousness and what appears as a 3-D physical world more from a psychological level. They have not yet understood that the fundamental structure of the universe is actually consciousness that is interactive.

Some advanced scientific researchers are starting to get a glimpse into the understanding that we live in a holographic universe. Yet having a mind that is not located in the brain, or even the concept of a soul that exists beyond the body, is a highly debated issue.

Increasingly, there is more and more proof from doctors, for example, who tell stories from their patients that have returned from the operating table. Already declared dead, these patients have full recall of events that happened in adjacent rooms. Others who were taken to higher dimensions were given profound information in order to come back here to Earth to tell us about it. I have interviewed and met quite a number of such people and they are all totally convinced that life goes on and that soul is a total reality.

Once you have advanced far enough on the path of communicating with the universe, you yourself are then able to prove the existence of your higher consciousness and the existence of your soul. You will know with 100% certainty that your mind, your consciousness, lives forever and does directly affect your body and the world around you.

Let me tell you a real-life story that shows how our focus can defy the laws of time and space. The following chapter "*Living in a Holographic Universe*" was published in the bestselling book **Success Blueprint**, which I co-authored with Brian Tracy and other thought leaders.

LIVING IN A HOLOGRAPHIC UNIVERSE

Let me invite you on a journey into a different kind of universe, one that allows for parallel universes to exist side-by-side. This story contains the secret behind how we create success.

Imagine you are sitting down in an airplane, a Boeing 777, with its small video-display right in front of you. To your right-hand side sits a pediatrician, who has taken this flight to Washington, D.C. many times, and he's on his way to give a lecture in D.C. You're on the flight to Key West, Florida to attend a conference and you have a short layover in Washington Dulles Airport.

However, instead of going to land in Washington, D.C., after flying in a holding pattern for half an hour due to thunderstorms, the captain announces that the airplane has been re-routed to Baltimore, Maryland.

The pediatrician next to you tells you with 100% certainty that this always happens, every single year, due to the weather in the summer on the East Coast. The pediatrician also tells you, in great detail, that you will be deplaning in Baltimore, Maryland, then you will be shuttled by bus back to Washington D.C., where you will most likely arrive much too late to catch your connecting flight. And worst of all, he makes the dire prediction that you probably won't even make your connecting flight until the next morning. He's been through it many times and he knows how it goes.

Even the small video monitor in front of you shows

you the new flight path now as a bright red line, heading straight to Baltimore, Maryland.

This can't be true! You exclaim in your mind. You need to be on time for the conference in Key West, as participants depend on you!

For some magical reason you had found a fascinating book in the seat pouch in front of you that you had started reading since take-off. It was about Time – Space –Shifts, and about Parallel Universes.

Based on the new understanding of quantum physics, you had learned that this universe is **consciousness interactive.** It appears to act much more like the *holo-deck* did for the crew of *Starship Enterprise.* For those who are not *Trekkies,* let's just say that the universe acts more like a holographic picture show in which your thoughts, your visions, and your focus, all become 3-D reality.

Needless to say, you had become very fascinated by the possibilities that quantum theory offered.

You had already been reading books about how success is created by having clear goals in your mind and by imagining a positive outcome.

You knew that you pre-create your success by imagining yourself in your own successful future in advance. You had already been practicing some of these steps in your own life and already created good results. And you felt you had mastered one of the master keys for creating your success in advance: To feel what it would feel like if your goals or wishes had already been realized and fulfilled. This brings about the creation of your success faster and with greater ease.

Landing in Baltimore, Maryland, as the flight purser had just announced, and being late for your conference, was just not an option. This book on Time – Space – Shifting and Parallel Universes had you intrigued and you were ready to try out some of the techniques outlined in the book.

Not taking no for an answer, you made yourself comfortable in your seat and simply closed your eyes. You knew that you needed to have a PERFECT BLUEPRINT in your mind before you can manifest the desired external result.

You started by imagining being at a beautiful beach. The anxiety began to leave your body and you started feeling much more at ease.

In your mind you now recalled the steps:

The first step is to STEP BACK, out of the picture of your current experience.

This allows you to TAKE A LOOK at the situation, as if you are outside of the problematic situation. And as you begin to get an overview of the situation you start feeling even more relaxed.

The second step is to define your goal. This way you start taking on the position of being the director of your own life's film, and you RE-FOCUS on what you REALLY want. To do this you DESCRIBE the goal clearly:

You land on time in Washington Dulles Airport in order to catch all your connecting flights, in order to participate at a conference in Key West, Florida, tomorrow.

The third step is to IMAGINE and FEEL exactly what it is

that you REALLY WANT as if it already had happened.

You imagine yourself arriving in Key West, just in time for the conference to start the next day.

You can already feel the warm, balmy air of Key West caressing your skin as you arrive on time. You can see how everything re-aligns itself perfectly.

In the last step, you feel the end result as having already happened! You continue holding the vision of your future fulfilled until you can feel manifestation of the final vision with a 100% certitude in your bones.

Since success is built upon success, it is best to start with small miracles and work yourself up to expressing greater visions in time. This builds self-esteem and helps you create trust that the universe is really listening.

These steps are creating the PERFECT BLUEPRINT for your SUCCESSFUL experience.

Let me fast-forward the movie for you and tell you how it went for me when I was in exactly that same situation. I did what I'd learned to do, in order to create success and results: I pre-envisioned the success, and also transformed any blocks that were in the way, such as negative beliefs, doubts or fears.

Obviously, this wasn't the first time I had re-envisioned my universe and tried my hand at shifting into a more successful parallel universe. Over time I had already built up a series of successes and was able to muster up enough certitude in my focus that day.

When we landed I was so sure that we were going to land in Washington Dulles, that I congratulated my husband who was sitting next to me before the announcement by the flight crew!

To my dismay the purser of the flight announced that we had just landed in Baltimore, Maryland!

This is not how it was supposed to go, I thought to myself!

The pediatrician next to me felt proud, because his prediction had come true, just like he had predicted it would. He preferred to believe in Murphy's Law.

Instead of being flustered and upset, I just closed my eyes again and re-created the future-experience that I really needed and wanted. "We do live in a holographic universe," I kept telling myself, "and many parallel dimensions exist." I continued in my mind, "My perfect parallel dimension in which I successfully land in Washington Dulles airport equally exists. Contrary to what it looks like, I am not really in a solid universe!"

You may want to know that our thoughts have not been able to be measured as of yet, but thoughts have been observed to have effect on our physical word. In the scientific community the idea of alternate universes was first proposed in 1957 by Hugh Everett III, a young Princeton University doctoral candidate and one of John Wheeler's students. He called it the "Many-Worlds Theory" and used it as an explanation as to why quantum matter behaves erratically.

At one of the Prophet's Conferences I had the privilege to share the stage with Dr. Michio Kaku, a physicist, professor and bestselling author. I was honored to be invited numerous times to speak alongside presenters such as the late astronaut, Edgar Mitchell and thought-leaders such as Barbara Marx Hubbard and Jean Houston. Michio Kaku said in *highly scientific* terms: "There are probably other parallel universes in our living room. There are vibrations of different universes right here, right now. We're just not in tune with them. This is modern physics. This is the modern interpretation of quantum theory, that many worlds represent reality."

Professor Steven Weinberg, who earned his Nobel Prize in physics in 1979 states: "There are an infinite number of parallel realities coexisting with us in the same room." He goes on to explain: "There are hundreds of different radio waves being broadcast all around you from distant stations. At any given instant, your office or car or living room is full of these radio waves. However, if you turn on a radio, you can listen to only one frequency at a time; these other frequencies are not in phase with each other. Each station has a different frequency, a different energy. As a result, your radio can usually only be turned to one broadcast at a time. But there are an infinite number of parallel realities coexisting with us in the same room, although we usually cannot tune into them."

In order to shift into an alternate outcome of a better kind, I took a few moments of deep relaxation, and started refocusing my mind again on the desired outcome of landing in Washington Dulles Airport. Creating a powerful blueprint of a future event takes a little practice. However, all of us create these blueprints, all of the time, mostly haphazardly. We manifest our expectations all around us on a daily basis, albeit mostly subconsciously.

Today I simply refocused on what I really wanted (and really needed) at this moment, which was to arrive at Washington Dulles Airport.

Just when I felt this feeling with 100% certitude in my bones that this possibility was real, the purser announced with a great surprise in his voice: "Dear Ladies and Gentlemen, I was just informed that we actually landed in Washington Dulles Airport!"

In jubilant joy I turned to my husband and shook hands with him in affirmation that parallel universes and time-space shifts do exist. We do live in a holographic universe, just like many scientists are trying to tell us now.

Imagine now that it was you who had just heard to your amazement that you had landed in exactly the reality in which you had wanted to land in. How would you feel?

What you had done was follow the simple steps of creating the BLUEPRINT of SUCCESS in your mind. Instead of being dismayed at reality around you, you simply acknowledged the fact that this universe is indeed much more mysterious than you could've ever dreamed of, and you refocused and imagined what was really important to you.

Life will hand us enough opportunities to refocus on what we really want. There are two options: We can either give up, and give in, or we can be proactive and pre-create life as we wish to experience it.

Let us review the five steps of creating a SUCCESS BLUEPRINT:

TAKE A STEP BACK from the event that isn't going exactly the way you want it to.

TAKE A LOOK at what is going on, to get an overview.

RE-FOCUS on what you REALLY want to experience.

PRE-IMAGINE your SUCCESS and what you really want to experience, **until you can really feel** this goal or wish being fulfilled, 100%.

Then LET GO and let the larger universe re-arrange itself for the highest good of all concerned.

I have been teaching this system of *Living From Vision®*, a course that teaches how to create from the inside out, successfully to business people, laypeople, therapists, teachers, children, teenagers, worldwide in 6 languages for the last 25 years. These laws are universal and point to radically new ways of understanding life.

Life will teach us, either by giving us pain when we are refusing to cooperate, or by giving us pleasure and joy when we are cooperating with life. Either way, we will learn and grow and expand beyond the horizon of what we thought was possible.

Our reality appears to be solid, but it is acting more like a dream. You are the director of your dream life, and you can create the kind of outcome that you really want.

In the process of discovering the laws of the holographic universe, you will probably discover that there is a greater source of life that is at the center of all creation. Some call it the Source of All That Is, some call it God, and some people simply call it the Life Force.

By learning how to cooperate with the higher laws of the universe, and connecting your goals with the highest source, you will discover that you are much more than a three-dimensional body. You are here on Earth to discover what this greater YOU is about. Your successes and failures are the feedback which life gives you in order to teach what works and what does not work.

In time, we realize that we are more akin to a light bulb in a projector which illuminates the film, rather than the actor in the film. To the degree that we learn to connect to a higher force, we awaken to the greater power within us, which in turn allows us to create more beauty, happiness and fulfillment.

The future has arrived, and you are one of the pioneers, learning how to co-create a shift in your time space reality with your consciousness. Welcome to the future! Let us create a better world for ourselves, our children and family and the world around us.

And foremost: Be the legacy you want to leave behind.

Now let me take you on another journey. Don and I were dreaming big, but how big that was going to turn out, we had not anticipated. We were wishing to find a Time Travel Machine.

SEARCHING FOR A

TIME -TRAVEL MACHINE

Don and I were about 10,000 feet above sea level in the Rocky Mountains. We had hiked for a while in order to reach a small grassy knoll where we wanted to go on a vision quest one sunny afternoon.

We lay down on our blanket and started staring into the brilliant blue sky. Not a cloud in the sky and the sky was truly the limit.

What would we do if we had 11 million US dollars, we asked ourselves? This was a large sum of money at the time and it was going to give us the canvas upon which we could draw our dreams.

The possibilities seemed endless. Each of us drew up gigantically huge dreams, some of which seemed so out of this world, that they were not realistically achievable.

When we shared with each other about our experience, we discovered that many of our dreams were similar. Both of us wanted a beautiful home, teach the world about spirituality, be enlightened, travel the world and teach while traveling. Most of all we wanted to find a time travel device.

We also wanted to see certain people whom we knew in the health field, become very well known, in order to spread their amazing healing methods. I can still recall the feeling of expansion that this imaginary number of dollars created in me.

These dreams set wind under our wings of what was possible. If we occasionally take time to dream big, to go beyond what we think is ordinarily possible and really discover our next level of passion and pursue our dreams, we will evolve with the wind of change more joyfully. I suggest you do this regularly.

Often people like to set out and get going early in life to pursue dreams that family or society has handed down to them. Get schooling, get a job, get married and have children, and pay the mortgage. Settling into a rhythm soon turns into a rut. And what happens next is that life often offers temptations to evade the monotony, or feeling the pain of not listening to our dreams any more.

We do need to be challenged to grow to be happy and to fulfill the nearly invisible script of our soul.

If we don't set the bar a little higher by ourselves and voluntarily stretch beyond our comfort zone, life will creatively give us those challenges. We are meant to grow and evolve. Our spirit needs it. We need to set ourselves some kind of goals that help us grow beyond our current limits.

If we avoid the messages of the universe, the whispers of our heart, and not follow our dreams, often times a kind of subtle pain sets in. It might possibly come as a dullness or, if we really don't listen, disease can set in to make us move, grow and evolve.

The best trick to evolve without pain is to do so willingly. Remember this one.

Though the saying goes "No pain, no gain" it is not true. When we listen to our dreams, listen to the whispers of our soul, and when we then act upon those impulses, we voluntarily stretch our boundaries and grow. By doing so we can voluntarily face fears, feelings of not being capable enough, or uncertainty. But given time, we will grow, and expand.

Studies in happiness have found that when we voluntarily expand to a greater version of ourselves than we have previously embodied, then we start entering a state of energetic flow. We are forced, in a way, to expand beyond what's currently comfortable and known to us. However, this very expansion gives us the feeling of happiness when we are involved in doing something that expands us beyond the current limits.

Don and I were doing this voluntarily. We listened to our heart's desire and dreamed of possible futures. Two magical things happened.

First, the dreams that we made up about other people which involved giving them large sums of money to make them more well-known started manifesting without the help of money. We were baffled. How could it be that something we envisioned for someone else simply started happening without the resources that we thought were necessary in order to get there.

This is a big secret of the universe. You can see the end result you wish for, and the means make themselves available, magically and miraculously.

So we learned the lesson that we don't always have to have the funds in order to co-create the reality we wish to have.

The second miraculous and shall I say, the turnaround in our life happened because we dared to dream so far outside of the box. If I had told anybody at the time what we were doing they would've surely left us alone.

We were really excited about time travel. As a matter of fact we set up a party to meet our future selves. The day prior to the party, a friend came by at 7 a.m. and knocked loudly at our door.

"This book fell off the shelves last night and I've been looking for it for 13 years. Since you've been talking about time travel I think you absolutely need to read this book. I think it fell off the shelf for you."

By 10 p.m. we had read the entire book to each other out loud. With pounding hearts we realized the incredible coincidence of having received this book the day before our future selves were to arrive.

In our mind we believed in external time travel. We believe that time travel will undoubtedly exist in the future.

If we were to set up a party at a designated point in time, we thought we would draw our future self to us back in time. Our future self would surely remember and would come to visit us.

Reaching out to the future and feeling it come into the now point is actually a real technique. I will share with you how you can literally create total and absolute miraculous experiences here on earth. It will show you that we are living in a Consciousness Interactive Universe, and that the more you wake up, the more time-space becomes illusionary.

However, the story of the book was about two soul-mates who had received the gift of a time travel belt. Needless to say, every time an argument ensued between the two of them, they would use the time travel belt to go back in time to eradicate the pain of confrontation.

Every time they went back just a little bit prior to the point in time when they had the argument, they reset the timeline but lost sight of each other.

The moral of the story was that using the time belt, avoiding conflict, and not dealing with life head on was actually detrimental to their magical soulmate relation-ship.

That was it!

We called our party off. Our soulmate relationship was more important than having the time travel machine delivered into our hands.

You might laugh right now and think of us as being naïve. We were in our twenties – how could we believe that such a thing could be possible.

But the rest of the story is even more magical.

We literally packed up and went into the desert of New Mexico and Arizona, on our way to California. We were still set to find a time travel device. What we found altered the path of our life, altered the path of thousands of people's lives and altered the path of our future as a collective whole.

I was 25 years old, full of zest for life and a complete belief that the universe was listening by now.

We were reading the book **_Mega Brain_** by Michael Hutchison and were on the lookout for some of these brain enhancement devices.

As we put out the call to find such devices, the universe replied. Miraculously we found people working in this field at an old friend's house, at their junkyard, the most unlikely of places.

But the most magical encounter was when we had come to Murrieta Hot Springs in California. It was the hotbed for polarity therapy, followers of the Surat Shabd Yoga, which means the "Union of the Soul with the Essence of the Absolute Supreme Being."

We had noticed that every time we tried to leave, something brought us back to the retreat center. We tried to leave for four days and made it out only a few miles when something else happened that brought us back.

Then it was Friday. For the life of us we could not figure out what we were meant to find there.

So we made a big declaration to the universe.

"Dear God, you have to show us what we need to know before 1 p.m. Friday afternoon or else we leave!"

We patiently waited, but nothing happened.

The clock was ticking and it was just about 1 p.m. when we decided to get a final juice drink at the health food bar before leaving for good.

A man with a long white beard and equally white hair served as. We asked him if he could tell us where to find a Lilly tank, a flotation tank developed by Dr. Jon Lilly, who had also done research on dolphins.

Flotation tanks were designed to allow people to get out of body, and we wanted to give it a try.

The man behind the bar wanted to take a look at the book we were carrying. He leafed through it with great interest and concluded with one large statement saying, "I know someone who has a device that can do all of this."

He told us, in no uncertain terms, that we absolutely had to see this person. He gave us his phone number and told us to call him right then and there.

With hindsight I can tell you this was one of the most decisive moments in our life so far.

We heeded the call, and made the appointment.

Don still remembers to this day, how the hair on his arms stood on end when the man opened the door.

He instantly knew that we would be working with him.

He invited us in and kindly asked us to wait a little while because he was just finishing up with his last client. It was a child who had come with his brother. His brother had had his toes crossed over. They were using this type of treatment as a last resort because nothing else had worked on his crossed toes.

Eager to learn what can be done with Radionics, we spent all afternoon with this man telling us the ins and outs of this quantum science.

He demonstrated a radionic instrument for us. He had taken a picture of each one of us and put it into the instrument and we got the great honor to be analyzed. Furiously rubbing on a sort of smooth plate until his finger stuck and turning dials it took him only moments to discover what was wrong with each one of us.

He told Don that the informational field around his vertebra T-7 was out of alignment, and that he would fix it momentarily if he wanted to.

Of course we agreed.

Equally just a few more moments later and Don felt this crackling in his back and pain was gone.

He took another look at me and discovered that my neurotransmitter informational fields were out of alignment.

No kidding. For the last four months I had worked myself to the bone, feverishly working at a project for around 18 hours a day or more. Sleeping very little, I had experienced a burn out.

It was part of the reason we went on this journey.

But how could this be? How could he know what was going on within me when I had not told him anything about myself? He'd simply taken a Polaroid picture, used this rather small instrument with a rubbing plate on it and knew more than anybody could probably find out by doing a blood test on me.

Mind you, even Wikipedia is labeling Radionics as pseudo-science and at best says *"The claims for radionic devices contradict the accepted principles of biology and physics."*

I think that's a very kind way of putting it. Presently accepted principles of biology and science are surely outdated. They always are.

In every century they become outdated and are always superseded by new information and greater understanding of reality. However, the pioneers rarely ever are accepted into the mainstream until enough people have had personal experience.

We didn't need acceptable principles of biology and physics. We were blown away by what the children had told us. The two young brothers had come for a number of treatments and they themselves had been witness to the effect of this treatment, where nothing else had helped them.

30 years later I can tell you now that it is hair-raising that Wikipedia only has this much to say about this field of some of the most advanced quantum technology on this planet.

Please do visit the website about the SE-5. http://www.se-5.com Read the free book about it, ***Regaining Wholeness Through the Subtle Dimensions,*** and discover for yourself a door that will allow you to peek into a multidimensional universe.

Shifting time-space, operating from the quantum hyperspace and affecting reality shifts in this dimension are real and happening. Pumpkins don't lie.

Remember my fascination with Findhorn?

Farmers in America, Mexico, China, England, and Germany have grown larger and healthier plants, fruits and vegetables without the use of fertilizers compared to plants grown with fertilizers and pesticides.

But alas, hyper-dimensional understanding of reality has not made its way into the mainstream. That's why you are reading this book right now. You are probably ready to walk through the veil into a new world where only the bold will go.

And bold we were. Don and I instantly decided to buy the SE-5 instrument and our life was changed forever.

After learning how to use the instrument and trying some experiments, one of the things we did with the SE-5 was to scan a map to see where we should live.

I asked where our most ideal place to live would be in regards to our spiritual evolution, our relationship as soulmates, as well as our business. I landed in the middle of the Puget Sound, right across from Warm Beach just north of Seattle.

However, since I didn't want to buy houseboat, we settled for a rental-house in North Seattle at the time.

Two years later Don and I were invited to a house-warming party on an island north of Seattle by a participant, an older, white haired lady, who had taken our meditation classes, which we held weekly free of charge in Seattle.

Visiting her for her party, we were so taken by the beauty of this island that we set out to look for land ourselves.

We didn't have much money, mind you, but we thought we should pretend we had some.

Let me just say we bought a piece of land. The realtor lady was surprised to hear that we were planning to build a geodesic dome and told us that right across from our very newly purchased lot of land there also was a geodesic dome. Right across from us was WARM BEACH.

"Oh my God!" I exclaimed, "That is exactly where we were going to live in the water, right across from Warm Beach!"

When I had dowsed for the best place for us to live, I had landed right in front of our current beach. The map I was using was not showing the islands, hence I landed in the water.

Miraculously we were guided to this island by the woman who had taken our meditation class. How could it be that I had found the best place for us to live by simply using a map, and an instrument with a sticky plate?

Later we got to know a neighbor living down the street named Bill Cox. He was finding water wells for the government, because their scientific engineers could not find water by conventional methods but he could, by using an ancient technique called dowsing.

The miracles we've seen, the double-blind studies that have been done, the ability to program holograms which then in turn create change in physical reality and the structure of fruits and vegetables and plants spoke for themselves.

Wikipedia really only reflects the current state of accepted theories. Sadly so, nobody can find much truth in there. Or should I say, perhaps the people who dwell within the mindset of the norm are not yet able to draw such higher dimensional realities into their field?

Our very own mindset allows doorways to open, that do not open for everybody. Information has to be able to be digestible. If one digests too much new information it can cause mental indigestion.

Powerful tools, things that can create miracles, have to be used and can only be used by people with an understanding of higher reality.

Needless to say, a lot of people on this planet are operating within a mental norm, a set of beliefs, that 100 years ago the mainstream thought were absolutely impossible.

When Don and I set out to find a time travel machine we were very serious. We definitely dreamt outside the box. We dreamt BIG. And what we got was way better than what we had bargained for.

I hope you do take the time to discover this field of Radionics and take a look at the research data, as well as read books about it. Radionics provides tools that prove the cutting edge scientific understanding. It's the answer to Einstein's puzzle of spooky action at a distance.

It started with our hike in the Rocky Mountains and our vision quest on the grassy knoll at 10,000 feet.

This journey of dreams took us through the deserts of the southern United States, and landed us in the Northwest Pacific of America.

Just in the last 2 years alone, as of my writing in 2017, researchers in China have performed experiments with verified hospital studies with 30,000 patients, using water that has been programmed with informational fields using the SE-5 1000. Healthcare for the poor was the motivating factor to pursue this type of technology and method. Healthcare for the poor is too expensive for the government in China and they needed to look for other options. These researchers have diligently provided research data and breakthrough understanding of how informational fields create gravitational fields and thereby create changes in the physical structure.

So I encourage you to take time out regularly, to dream big, to pursue the wildest dreams of yours, and to become a living legacy.

Your dreams can become real to you because some part of you has the ability to be a guiding light. If you can dream it, it can become real.

SELF HEALING THROUGH IMAGERY

Co-incidence is God's way of remaining anonymous
Albert Einstein

Don, my beautiful beloved husband, and I were trying to get away from our bustling *Shambala Oceanside Retreat* center on the north shore of Bali and our *Shambala Spa* in Ubud for a little while. As much as we absolutely love all the amazing souls we meet in Bali, there comes a time when we need time-out and time to be alone with each other. Having everybody know you, whether you know them or not, can be nice, however Don and I really wanted to hide out at a place where nobody knew us. We decided to take a trip to the promised white sand beaches of Lombok Island, just a short boat ride from Bali.

Arriving in a torrent of rain after a 5 hour boat ride over a wavy and rocky ocean, we were glad we had brought our own van. We had to make our way south through the night, while rivers were flooding the roads.

The next morning after our breakfast, replete with white toast and sugar filled, plastic packaged jam, and squealing Christmas songs playing over the loudspeakers in a Muslim country where the prayer calls came 5 times a day and massive amounts of trash was floating up onto the beach, I felt like I was NOT in the right place at the right time. It was an eerie feeling and I really regretted having left our own little Heaven on Earth at *Shambala*.

However, knowing that we do create our own reality, Don and I didn't get deterred. We sat down to do our

125

morning visioning, utilizing the LFV App, and envisioned being in Heaven on Earth.

On a whim, we booked a hotel further up north on Lombok Island, because the pictures looked pleasing, the price was in our budget, and we set out to drive north. We missed our turn despite using a GPS and went just a little too far. Suddenly we spotted a huge sign at the side of the road: *Ayurvedic massages and VEGAN food!* Just in time I realized that we had gone too far, turned around and found our hotel.

For dinner we wanted to try out the newly discovered vegan restaurant. Don and I have been vegetarians since about the age of 19. As we entered the calm oasis we were greeted by a beautiful, radiant woman dressed in a turquoise colored Indian sari. The equally radiant turquoise infinity pool with a stunning view of the ocean, the palm trees and the setting sun made us feel like we truly had entered into an oasis. We felt like we were at the right time in the right place.

As I introduced myself, I noticed that this woman in the sari had a German accent. Being German myself, I asked for her name in German. "My name is Daniela," she told me in German, "and you are Ilona Selke, right?"

"Yes," I replied, puzzled and a tad bit sad to have our anonymous trip already discovered. "I had emailed you about a year and a half ago about the LFV Course. I had wanted to upgrade my course, which still had cassettes. Remember?"

I did! "And just to let you know, out of all the books that I could take in my one suitcase, I have taken the book **Wisdom of the Dolphins** as I set out on my journey

126

to fulfill my dreams." She had read my book in 2002 and shortly thereafter also done the *Living From Vision®* course with one of our LFV teachers in Germany.

She proceeded to tell me her miraculous story. Daniela had been sick for 17 years and had gone from doctor to doctor with no success at all.

As a result of reading my book she got hope. She took some of the techniques that I described in the book and started applying them to herself. Next, by taking the LFV course in the foothills of the Alps, she started envisioning herself being healthy. One Christmas shortly after Daniela had started on her journey of seeing herself as healthy, strong and living her dream life, her mother gifted her with an amazing Christmas gift: A trip to Sri Lanka and a stay at an Ayurveda Clinic.

The renowned Dr. Indrajith Walawe (https://dr-indra-jith.com) was the doctor who treated her and her health transformed before her eyes. She continued with the daily exercises of the *Living From Vision®* course diligently and pre-envisioned her state of vitality. She told me that she still remembers the image in full color to this day. By creating the feeling and an image that represented the fulfilled feeling in advance, she created the blueprint for her health.

Now I was standing in front of her, radiantly alive and glowing. A light was shining from her eyes that let me know that she was connected to a higher source!

After hearing her amazing story, I took a moment to reflect on the impeccable arrangement of our meeting. Just days before, I had asked for a confirmation that I should keep going in my work. I wondered about my next steps in life. Should I start to retire? Should I keep going? If there was ever a sign that the universe wanted to give me to say KEEP GOING, it was this one.

How exacting must the universe be to have guided us to this place in time?!

We had booked the hotel on a whim. We had just missed our turn to the hotel, despite GPS, and by chance saw the sign for the Vegan Restaurant and Ayurveda Spa (www.devaya.online). How many people on this island had ever read my book, let alone done the LFV course, and created a miraculous healing? It was like we had found a needle in a haystack! This amazing, divinely coordinated coincidence filled my heart with wonder. Out of all the people who lived on this island, we drove straight to Daniela. We were in resonance with each other's vibration and therefore we met.

A greater force than our conscious mind coordinates our meetings. Once you set your goals and set up your ideal vibration doing whatever it is that really inspires you, you will find the fulfillment of your dreams. The magic of this universe is that it is listening!

This showed me how important all our little actions are. Whatever you do, say or think today will find its match in the world around you tomorrow. The people that persist and keep living in the direction of their dreams will succeed and live a life of miracles.

Since I had just started my own television show, I decided to do an interview with Daniela the next day for my Quantum Living Television Show which was aired on Woman Broadcast Television Network (WBTVN).

Daniela reiterated that all the positive changes in her life had come from the very fact that she had pre-envisioned her successes. By feeling the fulfilled feeling that she would experience, once she would reach her dream and her goal, she had arrived at her destination. Dr. Walawe had helped her and she was "incidentally" gifted a trip to see him, because she had set up the blueprint in her inner heart and mind. By doing the daily exercises of the LFV course she stayed with this blueprint in her mind long enough for it to manifest.

This universe precisely matches our vibrations. The images and feelings you hold within yourself are the blueprints for what you will come to see as the reflection in your real life.

Whether we know it or not, we co-create all the time. Often our goals are influenced from childhood programming or mass media or even past lives and our DNA history. We usually pick the fitting DNA from our soul's perspective and the law of resonance finds the matching parents. But the evolution of our soul makes the difference as to how the DNA is manifest and what you do with the pattern of your design.

In order to create more of what you really want, I urge you to remove yourself from the programming of media. Media sells on the basis of fear. That pulls our focus on what is not working, bad luck, punishment, pain and suffering. If you want to clear your mind, stop watching the media at least for a long period of time. You can always instruct the universe to give you the news that a necessary for you. When needed, you will find a headline, see a TV newscast if it is needed for your safety, evolution or wellbeing. I have never owned a TV since I was 16 years old.

TV and mass media programs our subconscious and makes it harder to steer into a positive direction.

Instead of being programmed by mass media, you can create a life of fulfillment, happiness and forward evo-lution by sitting at the steering wheel of your own life. Every single choice you make will become the stepping stone toward a greater and happier life.

THE LAZY MAN'S GUIDE

TO ENLIGHTENMENT

Whatever you are doing, love yourself for doing it.
Whatever you are feeling, love yourself for feeling it.
This too you can learn to love.

Thaddeus Golas

I love the book ***The Lazy Man's Guide to Enlightenment***
by Thaddeus Golas. He states that there are two fundamental states that determine how much pain or pleasure we experience. We all know these states very well.
One state is contraction and the other state is expansion.
When we contract, we become denser, tighter, more like
a billiard ball. However, the denser we become, the more
we bump into things. Friction is the result and we usually experience it as pain.

When we expand, we become more wave-like, and we
can embrace whatever is in front of us. Love and bliss are
the feelings we get when we expand. You can test this
concept out in your daily life.

When we encounter a situation, we either contract
away from it, or we open to it and embrace it.

How does contracting or expanding matter in regards
to manifesting your dreams?

Let me tell you a short story to illustrate the power of
resistance.

131

When I was 19, right after finishing high school, I started to work as a flight attendant for Lufthansa. I wanted to save money for my studies later on. My virgin trip as an active flight attendant took me to London. We stayed at a five-star hotel overnight. I still vividly remember sitting on my bed in a five-star hotel surrounded by posh furniture. I started crying.

"How did I deserve this?" I lamented. I cried over the luxury that was surrounding me. Now you might wonder why I would lament about luxury. However, at the time, my ideal future was studying at Cambridge as a poor female German student, living under the roof in the attics of some old lady's house.

As I used to do then and sometimes still do, I like to pick a book when I have a question and open it to an arbitrary page to see what the universe has to tell me. The book that lay on my nightstand that night in London was called ***The Lazy Man's Guide to Enlightenment*** by Thaddeus Golas. I opened to a random page seeking an answer as to why on Earth I was in the exact opposite reality than what I had dreamed up as my ideal future. I figured that the universe could give me answers in this oblique way.

"This too you can learn to love!" were the words that stared me in the face! The lesson struck like thunder. I had envisioned myself being a poor student. However what I experienced was the opposite. I abhorred the riches that surrounded me. And yet, that is what I created around myself. The message was loud and clear! Love what you resist, and it will dissolve. I quickly looked around the room and told every piece of teak furniture that I loved it. I got the message! The sooner I was able to love what surrounded me, the sooner such a lesson would no longer be needed.

Until we have learned to love what we resist and have transformed our inner little demons, we will get plenty of chances to learn to love. You might know the saying by C. G. Jung: What we resist, persists. He was referring to the suppressed parts of ourselves which unconsciously motivate us to "get away" from it. Later I will share with you a powerful technique I have taught clients around the world for the last 25+ years that will easily transform your shadows into powerful magnets of light.

As far as resistance goes, you may have noticed in your own life how resistance creates a sort of negative attraction. We often get exactly that which we have resisted. But the good news is: *You can learn to love it.* Whatever we yet have to learn to love, is usually what surrounds us, until we have transformed our resistances and start manifesting what we love.

Resistance is a form of contraction where we experience ourselves as separate and bump into the other, be it a state, a thing or a being. This causes friction and is usually experienced as unpleasant or even painful.

When we go into expansion and become permeable, we start to feel love. Any other solid form can be embraced by us and thereby does not create friction or pain. We might even go into union and feel a tremendous amount of positive feelings.

The greater your ability to become expanded, the greater is your feeling of love. Thaddeus Golas calls it *"the becoming a space being."* When you are becoming one with eternity, you are in the ultimate state of love and union. At a personal level, we are able to experience soul love and perceive ourselves as coming from the same soul. Hence the feeling of finding a soulmate.

Through this little story I wanted to illustrate to you how what we resist persists. How even our subconscious feelings, beliefs and attitudes of resistance run the show of our life from behind the scene. We may or may not be aware of all that we resist but that does not matter. This is the reason why some people get what they don't want.

The cure is that anytime you are faced with something that you are not enjoying, tell yourself that *you can learn to love this too*. Notice how wonderful this thought alone makes you feel. Soon your expansion and love will melt the resistance like ice melts in the sunshine and gives way to your intentional positive creations.

Naturally when you learn to love something, you can then either live with it or not and you will not be bothered by it. What matters most is that you are free to create what you want, and not what you don't want.

STORIES OF SMALL MIRACLES

Let me share some stories of people who have manifested a number of miracles while using the power of their imagination and the Living From Vision® course. This will serve you to get inspired to create your own prayers to be fulfilled and create your own miraculous life. Remember that all these people did was to connect, through their inner focus, with a power greater than themselves to create a life of miracles.

GETTING A BOOK CONTRACT

This story is about a German author, Thomas Goerden. By now he has become a well-known author. But at the time, sometime in the mid-1990s, he was still in the beginning of his career. I met him because he had been assigned to translate my book Wisdom of the Dolphins into German by the Heyne publishing company. To prove to himself that the book he was translating was indeed worthy, he decided to take the LFV course with Marion Selke. She was his LFV teacher and coach during his five-week journey in order to see what miracles he could create for himself.

He himself had just written a novel and was hoping to find a publisher. During the first session he was prompted not only to imagine his wish fulfilled, which was a publishing contract, but Marion also encouraged him to be specific and to write down how much money he wanted to get and by what date he wanted to receive his confirmation. Thomas wrote down the amount of money he wanted for the contract with the publisher and the date by when he wanted to hear about it. Daily he visualized getting the contract on time. He was diligent in his daily "homework". Mornings and evenings, he listened to the LFV audio exercises and he also followed the advice his own inner images gave him. There was partly the inner work, and also partly the outer work based on his insights.

Almost beyond his expectation, he received a letter from a publishing firm. Magically it was on the very day which he had set for himself as a target. And to make him even more amazed, he not only received the very contract he had hoped for, albeit by a different publisher than he had thought, but also the exact amount of money he had wanted.

PHANTOM OF THE OPERA – a small miracle!

There was a woman who took a course with one of the LFV teachers in Germany.

She wanted to hear the music of "The Phantom of the Opera". She had set four goals, and this particular goal was the smallest one, but she reasoned that it was better to build successes and to grow over time in her abilities to create miracles. I like that approach as well. A mixture of some smaller and some grander wishes is a good mixture. It gives us the chance to reap the rewards sooner, learn about what did work and start feeling greater trust and success sooner. But seeing larger goals manifest is often more life-changing. They are meaningful to our growth because we need to stretch our inner concepts and beliefs about what can happen. We need to address the way we "are" in order to accommodate the manifestations of larger goals. Those larger goals help us grow into a greater being.

Here is how this woman created her first miracle. The first evening of the class she was asked to choose her four goals for the coming five-week course. She was led through a series of exercises to set up the mental image, the fulfilled feeling, and the metaphorical image for her goals. She felt all of her wishes being fulfilled during one of the guided imagery exercises.

When she arrived home just a few hours later, she was in for a surprise! On her kitchen desk she found the Phantom of the Opera CD – her daughter had bought it for her that very afternoon! This woman had no idea that her wish would be fulfilled so quickly. She had simply pre-created the blueprint inwardly and thereby opened the doorway to shift into the world where this wish was a living reality.

From our perspective it looks like the wish has a three-dimensional way to manifest. What our eyes don't see is that we actually only shift into one of the many available realities and occupy it. All we need to do make a choice as to what we want to create and the universe re-creates itself around us. It is postulated that in a civilization that is thousands of years ahead of us, all inhabitants are able to time shift, to traverse space instantly and to enter through the wormholes of time. Currently we are only able to teach these methods to relatively few on this planet that already are ahead of the general mass consciousness.

To direct the mind, especially the subconscious mind, gives the universal energy a river bed to flow into. Water that would be poured onto a flat surface would have less power than water poured into a river. Our attention, our wishes, create the river bed. That is all we need to do.

MANIFESTING AN AUDI CONVERTIBLE

Some years ago a German filmmaker came to one of my seminars, learning about shifting the patterns of the subconscious mind. He got enamored with this process and soon became an LFV teacher. During his very first class, he wanted to really prove the methods to himself. He decided to manifest a car in five weeks or less. Not just any car, it was a blue Audi convertible sports car, costing a sizable amount of money. And he wanted it brand new. Every day he followed the daily audio exercises in the course, visualized his goal, felt the feeling he would have if he already had his wish fulfilled and imagined the finalized metaphor that represented the feeling. Interestingly it is not the car he visualized, but the feeling he would have if he drove his very own Audi convertible. This feeling of freedom he imagined to have, was best represented by a white dove.

It is the fulfilled feeling we want to get from our wishes. What fulfills us is not the thing, in and of itself. The fulfillment comes from the feeling that a book contract, the money, the car or the CD give us. The fulfillment of a wish gives us a feeling inside our heart and soul. We can't really do anything with the "things" but we will feel a certain way, once we experience them. THAT feeling is what we aim for.

Remember that point because it is crucial to understanding how to manifest and how to navigate through inner dimensions, negative emotions and how to create time and space in alignment with your inner light.

Barely three weeks after he had started the LFV course, he received a call from Lotto Totto, a German lottery. "Hello Mr. we want to let you that you won an Audi convertible!"

"Oh," he exclaimed in joy, "Tell me, what color is it?"

"It will be red," the friendly voice replied.

"Oh, no!" he thought, "I had hoped it would be blue!"

Not long after, he invited us to test drive his car in Wiesbaden, Germany to give us a three-dimensional experience of his dream come true! He had simply celebrated the feeling of freedom that he had visualized every day for three weeks, in the form of his white dove flying freely.

In fact one of the secrets of manifesting is that the universe gives us more of what is already there. This applies to either positive or negative focus. Whatever we "hold" in our energy field, in our thoughts and hearts, whether conscious, subconscious or superconscious, it will duplicate itself into our 3-D world.

Therefore, it is absolutely necessary to pre-experience our wishes as already fulfilled – even if just for minutes a day – in order to see them manifest in the outside 3-D world.

By experiencing the fulfillment internally ahead of time, you are independent of the outer world and independent of the outer circumstances. You can create what you want inside. Once you have a satisfied feeling inside of yourself, you already feel the satisfaction. You no longer need the outcome. Yet we see that this is exactly what ensures that the result will come about. It is a paradox in a way. This is one of the most essential aspects to consciously creating. Once you no longer need something, you are free to receive it. It is as if God, or the universe, will only return to us into form, what we are able to let go of. Once we let go of the urgency or the feeling that something is not there, we open the current for that something to become embodied in our 3-D world.

You can also see it another way. You get what you feel is yours already. By feeling that state in advance, the change is already present in your aura.

This is how you set up a resonant field, a field of energy that will duplicate itself in 3-D. It is a law of the universe: "As above, so below."

Due to the law of resonance, all things that are vibrating similarly will resonate with each other. Whether it is the E-string on a piano that makes all other E-strings on the piano start to hum along once it is struck, or whether it is walking into a room of happy people which start making you feel happy too, is based on the same law: The law of resonance.

That means that conversely when you set up a field of energy, the resonant pattern will find its way to you. All things are inter-connected at a higher vibrational reality in a field of unity. This state is beyond the capacity of western measurement, a realm higher than we can see with our physical eyes.

Create your inner heaven first and your outer heaven will follow.

The white dove, which the film maker from Germany

140

was using to represent owning the car, was the bridge towards manifesting his goal.

AN ORPHANAGE IN INDIA

A Naturopathic doctor once took the LFV class which was being taught by an architect and his wife in northern Germany. In his first session, this doctor set an ambitious goal as he wanted to test the truth of using his higher mind to co-create miracles. He wanted to manifest more land for his orphanage in India. In effect, he needed about 100,000 USD in order to buy an adjacent piece of land and to build school buildings on it. He wanted to see his wish fulfilled within those five weeks that he was taking the LFV course.

Faithfully he focused his mind every day, morning and evening, on his goals and energized the wish fulfilled. He also practiced a new self-image he created for himself during the course, in order to become more like his higher self. One day during the third week the doctor had the insight to approach a large chemical firm in Germany about his goal. Low and behold, after his presentation of his dream, that very firm donated almost 70% of his desired total amount!

The other 30% was donated to his project during the next two weeks before the end of the course. This doctor had a mindset to help others. Although his goal was rather large and looking at it from a "normal" perspective, highly unlikely to manifest, he was able to manifest a large sum of money fairly quickly. We see this quite often when a person is asking for something that fulfills a greater sense of purpose. He was not just manifesting out of greed, he was working for the good of the whole.

When you wish for something that is in alignment with your soul's wish you will find unbound resources at your fingertips. When we work with a sense of purpose and service, we can step out of the way and allow the higher forces to fill in our gaps. When we feel in touch with the source and our higher self, the flow happens.

Learning how to manifest will work miracles on your entire being, and not just get you more material goods. This is not about a push-button method that delivers goods to you. Instead, learning to manifest is a journey of evolution. As you focus on things to come in a positive way, you will focus and connect with the higher universal light. You will start to communicate with your own higher center, your soul, in order to connect to the center of creating. This in turn will further your evolution to become a being of a higher order.

As part of becoming the next evolutionary level of human being, the "Human Divinicus", we increasingly learn to understand the secret workings of the universe. We are here to realize the powerful connection to God, or whatever you want to call that mysterious force that imbues everything with life and consciousness, and you become a conscious co-worker with it.

All through the ages we have received teachings that remind us to claim our birthright. Each religion, at its core, teaches us of the connection to a higher source. They all teach that thoughts create reality and can affect miraculous change in time-space. They teach in so many words that we co-create reality with our full attention! Whether the Bible talks about prayer, or the yogis who are trained to enter the deepest levels of consciousness to manifest the various powers of vibhuti, it all points towards the same evolutionary step: To consciously align ourselves with the higher forces that surround us everywhere and become the next evolutionary expression of the Homo Divinicus. We might call it the Full Potential Human.

The laws are imperceptible and only through trial and error, through feedback from real life, do we learn how to navigate to a higher order of creating.

We all live in a school house called Earth. Grade upon grade we raise our ability to understand. Our understanding of the subtler and less obvious laws of life becomes easier and easier.

Your choice is what matters in every moment. Whether you create or manifest something wonderful or whether a moment arises that is challenging such as a car cutting in front of you, or a worker not being able to fulfill his promises on time, it is your own attention that helps make the difference. Do we use our attention to bring about a better situation, or do we use our attention to see the worst come true?

Each situation in our lives allows us to choose!

Floating in Air

In China, until not too long ago, a Chinese doctor was trained to see into the heart of their client's health issues in the first two minutes they met. I once met such a trained doctor from China. He was famous for getting people out of long comas, even when western medicine had failed.

143

He looked at my hand and then proceeded to tell me all my childhood issues, my parent's issues, as well as what will happen to me later in life. About all the things in my past he was 100% right.

He told me that his own grandfather and friends of his grandfather were able to float in space, back in the time when he was still a child. They were practicing Spiritual Boxing, which allowed them to inhibit bleeding from sword wounds, as well as the ability to float. Such people live even today.

With training, we can all supersede current laws of physics and see into the past and future. As you raise your vibration you will also learn to adjust time-space and create more beauty, health and vibrancy in your life.

BALI WOMAN WHO CURED HER STOMACH

We had been living in Bali (7 months out of the year) for a several years and my Indonesian had become good enough to guide meditations in Indonesian. I had a favorite wood furniture maker and I visited him on and off on my way from our Shambala Retreat Center to our Spa in Ubud.

On one such day I was shocked to see the wife of the wood-worker. She had become ghastly thin and looked very ill in health. I asked her what was going on and she told me in great detail her predicament. She had stomach ulcerations which she was eager to show me on photos which had been taken of her internal stomach. Due to these ulcerations, she was not able to eat much at all and had lost too much weight. She looked pale and hopeless.

144

I really didn't know what to do for her physically, so I resorted to telling her that her mind and prayers were all-powerful. Since the doctors felt that they could not help, there was not much to lose. I told her to sit every morning for five to ten minutes in meditation and to imagine her stomach fully healed. I told her with the authority of a western woman who teaches people all over the world that she had to imagine the perfect end-result: a healthy inner stomach lining!

I told her to do this positive imagery exercise, much like a prayer, for a few months and that this seeing the end-result was the magical ingredient to creating miracles. Being in Bali I knew that the belief was still very strong among the Balinese people. Here miracles are still plentiful and stories abound. This woman had a good chance to mobilize her inner healing abilities.

Lo and behold, when I visited her and her husband about six months later, she greeted me in full radiance. I was taken aback. In a way, I had dreaded to go see them but here she was, fully healed.

I asked her what had happened and how she had healed. She had gained her weight back, her sunken eyes had returned and her face looked young again. She told me in full excitement that she had followed my instructions fully and that it had turned her health around. Her husband had also started to sit in silence and to do his form of prayer and meditation every day. Furthermore, I saw him a few weeks ago on another visit, and he had lost some extra weight he was carrying and was looking radiant. He had become a vegetarian and was connecting to the higher source within. The proof was in their radiance that had returned. Not only did they both become healthier again, they also looked more in love and in harmony!

Our smallest change in habits can affect all other areas of our life. And by changing ourselves, we affect the world around us and those that we touch.

WOMEN LOSE WEIGHT

A brand new LFV-teacher was going to offer her virgin class in Cologne, Germany to a group of women who all wanted to lose weight. This new teacher, a woman in her mid-thirties, wanted to see how affecting a change in the inner world could be used to affect changes in the body. The task was not to watch the food consumption like in dieting, but to create four goals around the end-results which weight-loss would bring about.

These women picked goals such as: looking attractive in new beautiful clothing, feeling and being fit, having endurance or whatever sport qualities they wished for, etc. The women chose to focus on the end-result image of themselves. Their new Ideal Self-concept and greater confidence filled the four goals that each participant chose. Each morning and evening they focused on the fulfilled feelings and images that they each had chosen for each of the four goals.

Within five weeks, not changing their diet, they had all lost weight. It was not what they ate that needed the focus. Their subconscious mind and the universe at large needed to know what the end-result was to look and feel like.

GETTING PREGNANT

One couple had tried to get pregnant for over 10 years and were suffering from never having succeeded. They had given up hope. When they decided to take a Living From Vision® class together as a couple they wanted to improve their relationship. However, when their teacher told them to dream big and to go for their deepest passion, they decided to choose having a baby as one of their four goals. As you may well know, when you choose something, the universe will come up with its own way of making such a request happen. This may not be the way that we thought it would happen. Sometimes the solution comes about in a very different way than we might have imagined. This couple was open to any which way the universe could fulfill their dream.

Over the five weeks that it took to complete the course, they took time to share with each other and to re-invent themselves as a couple, as well as individuals. They also both imagined having a baby.

In a letter, back at a time when we all still wrote physical letters, they invited Don and myself to visit them at their home in order to see the result of the LFV course with our own eyes.

Despite all odds they had indeed gotten pregnant! After ten years of trying to get pregnant without any results, they were blown away by the power of their imagination. They both had created a blueprint for the universe to fulfill. They dared to dream big and the universe listened. We are the architects of our lives. Whatever we thought we couldn't do, we can turn around if it is our passion. With perseverance and listening to the universe's feedback, we will encounter miracles, experience greater vistas, and discover new horizons.

Manifest we will, small or large, unconsciously or consciously, painful or happy outcomes; the sky is the limit.

When we understand that we are the co-creator of the life we live, that we are the directors of our lives and that the universe is ever-ready to pour life force into our dream, that is the moment when we take on greater roles in the spectrum of being human. The more we learn and understand to activate our higher human capacities, the more we are functioning as beings of a higher order.

The physical laws can be defied, as many stories about yogis have described. Time and space work according to the vibrational frequency you occupy. When you shift your vibrational pattern, and supply a blueprint, you will experience a different reality.

RAIN IN HAWAII

I had fallen in love with a Bali couch and we purchased it for our little Hawaii house. It was slated to be delivered on a Friday evening, after hours, at 7 p.m. It had been pouring buckets all day but I thought it would eventually stop. By 6 p.m. it was still pouring rain and I started to get concerned. Our living room was on the second floor and the couch, made from teak wood, was heavy and certainly would not be easy to carry up the steps. In desperation, I stood in our living room, staring out the sliding glass doors at the gloomy sky. Closing my eyes I connected with the clouds and started pleading with them. "Could you please not rain when the couch is being delivered," I asked. "Well, you should have asked us sooner. We are loaded up with rain. No chance to stop so quickly!" I nearly heard them reply. (Ok, it was telepathic, but we do translate meaning into words in our mind, so this was the equivalent).

The clouds were right. I was a bit late in my request.

"I see," I replied.

Instantly I knew how to fix that problem. Time nor space are truly fixed constants, in as much as physics is still trying to tell us. Time is variable and depends on the frequency at which you vibrate. If you move faster in your core vibration you can reach into the past and future. Yogis, psychics and other extraordinary beings have seen the future and into the past for ages. We know from miracle stories that time and space has altered when people really needed miracles.

My solution was to raise my vibration. Or as I imagined it, to rise up along an imaginary beam of a time line. Much like Einstein traveled on a beam of light and got his famous E=mc2formula for the speed of light, I rose to a higher altitude, so to speak, when I vibrated to a higher time-space coordinate. In our consciousness we can encompass greater time-space the higher you rise. If you go to the very center of creation, the universe, or God, you touch or become eternity.

I didn't rise as high in my frequency so as to touch eternity, but just high enough to reach the clouds a few hours earlier. I needed to deliver my request at an appropriate time, so that the clouds had time to adjust, and stop raining by 7 p.m.

Hovering at this higher speed in my inner mind, being back in time by choice, I asked the clouds again if they were willing to stop raining at 7 p.m. in time for our delivery. I flashed my need for a dry staircase into the mind of the clouds. This time, lo and behold, they understood me. Apparently the "Now" which I had arrived at, was just far enough back in time for the clouds to adjust their heavy load. "Ok," was their answer, "we can do that!"

I was delighted! The clouds talked to me and promised cooperation!

I can't tell you if rising up higher in time to an earlier point in time was allowing me to believe that it was possible for the clouds to stop raining by 7 p.m., or if my imaginary journey to a higher frequency of time, one which allowed me to speak to the clouds at an "earlier" time was real. But what really mattered was what happened next.

It kept raining buckets for the next hour with no end in sight. Just minutes prior to 7 p.m., the delivery truck drove into our driveway. The rain had not stopped, like they had promised me that they would. What would we do? Would they carry the couch in pieces over the slippery wooden staircase? Would we all get soaked to our bones? Would it be safe?

The truck came to a stop, and the driver opened his doors. I already had umbrellas in hand, ready to go downstairs to meet the driver when, as if on cue, the rain stopped! What!? The rain simply had stopped!

"Did they really hear me?" It certainly looked like they had.

For the next 45 minutes we carried all the pieces for the Bali couch up the stairs and put the couch together. I loved it. I didn't know at the time that later in my life I would have a lot more amazing Bali couches. For the time being I was in heaven! No sooner did the driver put his shoes back on, and we opened the sliding glass door, that the rain started to pour down again!

THE SHAMAN FROM NEPAL

Recently, a friend of mine who guides treks into Nepal for a few months every year told me that he witnessed a Shaman who looked like he was floating before his very his eyes. To make sure it was not a trick on his mind, he took some photos. He was permitted to do so. On the photo, instead of legs one could only see smoke at the bottom of his body. When the same Shaman was standing between two Western men, the photo showed the two men and some smoke between them instead of the body of the Shaman.

This Shaman had learned to raise his vibration to such a level that to our physical senses he no longer appeared solid in his 3-D body, not in reality to my friend's eyes, nor on the photo. We may think that we have one single physical world. However, the world consists out of many layers of frequencies simultaneously.

That is the nature of life here on Earth. We live in a spectrum of frequencies. What we can learn to do is master our frequencies. Manifesting a parking lot is one step. Manifesting anything that you wish for is to realize the powerful connection between our dreaming mind and the 3-D world. In the end we realize that all there is, is consciousness.

151

By raising your awareness to the singular point and entering your soul consciousness and refining this, will bring about a greater brilliance in your daily life. All areas of your life will start to reflect the purity of your subconscious, of your emotions, your ethics, and indeed you will become pure, with pure expression in your words, deeds, and thoughts. This is a road so ecstatic with untold mysteries to unravel, with ecstasy as your reward.

DISCOVERING PERFECT TIMING

A female psychotherapist and reader of my book Wisdom of the Dolphins, had signed up for a number of my workshops, as well as the LFV self-study course in Germany. She loved the techniques and started dreaming big. Her daily life was already pretty spectacular, but she had set her mind on living in a more magical world. One day she told me, "Ilona, I want to live like you, under palm trees, by the ocean with dolphins!" She used the LFV course to visualize her wish fulfilled and was diligent with her homework, doing each of the daily audio exercises that follow along with each week of the course material.

After one year she called me, a little perturbed. She had been doing what it takes and yet her wish had not manifested. She was disappointed.

She invited Don and myself to her home and we shared a fabulous dinner. I was inspired by her interior design, so daring, so vibrant. Her husband was a public figure in the entertainment world and was getting sacks full of fan mail weekly.

I got to see her life first-hand. She proudly showed me the photos of her eldest son who was seventeen at that time, and raved about the adorable relationship he had with his younger brother, a boy age four at the time. Both of them, so she told me, were inseparable.

"What is going to happen to them when you get your wish of living under palm trees and by the ocean?" I asked her. Presumably they would have to split up and the older boy would have to stay in Germany to finish school and the other boy, who was not yet in school, would be flexible.

I looked at the energy and bond that the two brothers shared and turned to her and said, "Give it two years. In two years' time the older boy will be nineteen and done with his schooling. He will have to do social services or military services (which was still required in Germany at that time) and then he will move out of home."

"And the younger boy," I continued, "will be starting school in two years. At that time he too will become more independent and the two will naturally go their own ways. They will naturally give up the tight bond they were sharing and it will be OK for you to move house and hearth to make your dream come true."

Timing is everything. Sometimes our wishes involve other members of our family and naturally we are bound by their needs and our desire to respect their needs.

Indeed, in two years' time, a miracle happened. She and her husband were able to purchase a piece of land on an island, directly at the ocean with palm trees over-head and dolphins that swam by.

Our deeper desires include the wellbeing of others. This balance of timing of our wishes, desire and needs can be understood better from a higher perspective, which we are granted to see at times.

Conversely, we need to honor the wishes of others in our life and make sure that we co-create our reality in harmony with them or the greater whole. Remember what Don told me, when I was wanting to manifest that my husband was in total harmony with my spirituality and sexuality? He told me not to put a face to my wish. In the end, a new man, Don in this case, took up the place of being my husband who fulfilled all what I held dear in my heart.

A mother in India took the LFV course and her primary wish, she confessed, was to see her daughter married. As it was culturally still the habit in India at that time, the wish of the parents superseded the wish of their children. However, I acquainted her with the principle of creating happiness from within, rather than depending on outer circumstances to bring this happiness to us.

Furthermore, we can better tolerate others and their right to learn from their own mistakes by imagining this scenario:

If a dictatorship-type cool yogi with an all-powerful mind one day decided he had had it with wars and was only allowing peace on Earth for all, and from then on we were only permitted to experience harmony, you might quickly understand that free will and the natural law of resonance are already miraculous. Many people are at times horrified about politicians, and wars. But could you imagine that there is a need for those lessons?

It might not be yours. You may be able to see the freight train coming from far away, hear its noisy horn ahead of time and get out of the way. You may not need certain lessons, but that does not mean that others don't.

Instead of worrying that we are coming from ego-driven wishes and fret over manifesting a life according to our whims, we can stipulate to the universe that whatever we wish for will only be supported when it is in harmony and for the best of all concerned.

I tell God all the time only to support those wishes of mine which are in harmony with the good for all concerned and to cancel any wishes that don't serve the whole.

When we have this disclaimer in our formula of manifesting, we can rest assured that we have a karma free creation. A life full of miracles can be ours simply by starting to live to a higher tune. Life does work easier and with more pleasure when we attune ourselves to a level of reality of a higher order.

Sometimes it even seems like God, or the universe, is creating a plan for us. It is as if hands from a higher dimension are creating experiences for us.

In the next chapter, I take you to Hawaii again, this time to a moment in time before we magically found our house there.

CO-CREATING WITH THE UNIVERSE

If you recall from my second book *Dolphin, Love & Destiny*, I described that back in the 1990s we were looking to build a retreat center in Eastern Washington. Well, our vision went through a number of changes before it manifested when we least expected it.

Living in an intentional community was a popular idea and Don and I dreamed of living with like-minded people – imagine a Harry Potter school and people with superhuman abilities all living in one place. As if guided by an invisible hand we had found a community planner, a man named Larry who had helped countless intentional communities to flourish using permaculture principles. On a long drive to Eastern Washington, where we went to look for suitable land, Larry told us many secrets to creating a thriving community.

One such secret was that communities needed a common focus. When a group of people share a business plan, much like a wheel with spokes, everyone has a place within the structure, and everyone is needed to make the entire structure work. Another option he told us was to have a lead figure, a guru, or otherwise revered head of the group. Don and I quickly realized the pitfalls of such an endeavor, and, faced with certain winter blizzards, and the mud in the spring from melting snow, we realized that we would rather live by a dolphin beach by ourselves for now.

A couple of years later, we went to Hawaii to do an

interview for my book **_Wisdom of the Dolphins_**, with Roberta Goodman, who had been a dolphin assistant researcher with Dr. John Lilly. He was the famous doctor that had invented the floatation tank (also called the Lilly Tank) and was one of the foremost researchers in the medical field who said publicly that dolphins possessed a significant amount of intelligence. In fact, bottlenose dolphins, like the ones that look like Flipper, have a brain that is about 30% heavier and bigger than ours. Their brain also has more complex folding in the neocortex which is associated with abstract thinking.

Lilly, whom I was lucky enough to meet at his 81st birthday party on Maui in 1996, felt that essentially, we could only use telepathy to accurately understand the dolphins. Their way of thinking superseded that of linear logical thought, which is expressed in language.

In Roberta's house I happened to glance at a real estate booklet offering a house for sale at a very low price located by the beach. The house was located in an alternative community which was only using solar power for electricity at that time. I was excited. "An affordable house right next to a dolphin beach!" I told Don, jumping up and down. "Let us go see it." We decided to postpone our departure and drove to the house the next day with a real estate agent. The house was indeed only a few blocks from the dolphin beach, one of the few in all of Hawaii that dolphins frequent. *This is my day*, I thought. We found out that the man living here was an ardent follower of a linage of Indian Masters whose linage Don and I had followed. Everything looked good, but we just didn't like the style of the house.

Realizing that we do need to let the universe know

what we are truly passionate about, I exclaimed to the real estate agent: "I really want a house like the octagon house next door!" I particularly liked that the rain gutters were painted purple. She assured me that there was not another octagon available.

Well, I thought, *if there isn't one here, let us build one.* And unabashedly walked over to the realtor's big real-estate book which was lying on the hood of her truck. I opened it like I had opened my book **The Lazy Man's Guide to Enlightenment,** expecting the universe to provide some deep insight. To my surprise, right in front of my eyes I looked at a picture of an octagon house for sale and even cheaper than the one we were looking at!

"My God," the agent exclaimed, "that house is located only a few blocks from here. I can't believe it!"

We went to see the house immediately and decided to buy it right then, on the spot. The house was not completed, but did have the roof on and most of the windows. Even though it was just the shell, we loved it. It bordered a protected state forest reserve of flowering Ohia trees (which can live up to 600 years) and it was located just a few blocks from one of the only swimmable dolphin beaches in Hawaii.

A couple of months later, we flew back to Hawaii from our home in Washington to remodel the octagon house. Within three weeks we created an off-the-grid, fully self-sufficient house. We had solar electricity running my washing machine and vacuum cleaner, as well as a rain catchment system which provided our drinking and other water. Later we added an aqua-ponic garden where we grew salads and veggies. Over the following months we created a permaculture garden with many different types of fruiting trees. It seems supernatural to have finished our house in those three weeks. We did hire a lot of people, and our house was akin to a beehive for those three weeks. Our new neighbors were beyond belief – things just didn't move that fast in Hawaii. It was much like watching a time-lapse film of our house being finished. How can I explain the speed at which our house was built?

Before flying to Hawaii to remodel our new house, we had used the daily morning and evening exercises from the *Living From Vision®* course. We visualized our house being completely remodeled in our mind's eye, every day.

We created a blueprint much like an architect does.

Once we arrived on Hawaii, it seemed that everything was going as if in a miracle show. As our house was being built, it looked like a miracle show. In Hawaii, things naturally move slower, due to the tropical environment. But this house nearly built itself.

To our great amazement our new house was also located next to a retreat center, called *Kalani Honua*, which means *"Stairway to Heaven"*. It was directly on the other side or the forest reserve that bordered our land. Everything was within walking distance: The retreat center, the dolphin beach and an amazing community.

We realized that we didn't need to build our intentional community anymore because we had moved right into one. We were surrounded by people of all walks of life. They were living an alternative lifestyle, loved to swim with dolphins and many adhered to permaculture principles. And now we could teach seminars right next door, at *Kalani Honua*, a stairway to heaven.

Our passion, when we follow it, will find the perfect resonant field for us. Coordinated from a higher level we will find the right people, get the right insights and find the right help even while we are sleeping. What you create inside your mind is a blueprint. The necessary ingredients like the fitting people, connections and timing, all come in its perfect time once you have pre-created your reality from the inside out.

TRANSFORMING SELF-DOUBT

By now you definitely know that what you focus on is what you get. Spending your thoughts and feelings in the direction of your dreams is a far more effective way to arrive at your destination, rather than thinking of all the things you don't want. Have you ever seen anyone being able to drive their car by looking into the rearview mirror? By looking at what one is getting away from, one does not help you arrive at the desired destination very easily!

We need to look forward to where we are going. Furthermore, we need to know where we are going in the bigger picture. Having a road map, a larger vision is the best way to arrive at the life of your dreams.

Finding what you are truly passionate about, something you would do whether money was involved or not, is the key to activating your life's purpose. On a day to day level, you will find the energy to manifest your dreams when you pick something that makes your soul sing. Choose a path and dream that you are excited about and truly come from your heart. Many of our dreams were pre-digested and pre-selected by our family or our culture.

But how do we live our purpose? What is this mysterious purpose? How do we discover it? Many people have no idea what their life's purpose is and they desperately wish to find it.

To describe how to find your life's purpose and further-more how to transform any lingering negative self-image or low self-esteem that are often in the way, I want to tell you a story. Let me share some step by step tools that you can use to transform negative thoughts or feelings that might be in your way.

This particular technique that I love to teach the most, is based on Dr. Vernon Woolf's work called *Holodynamics*. It is based on the understanding that we live in a holo-graphic universe and when you make changes in your in-ner pattern of energy, you will see the reflection around you. As above, so below. As within, so without.

During a weekend seminar in northern Germany about 1994, I needed a volunteer in order to demonstrate how to transform negative beliefs that were in the way of living one's life purpose and passion. I was going to demonstrate the amazing *Holographic Transformation Technique* that we use to shift negative feelings and outdated beliefs. Once we transform our old patterns of beliefs, emotions and thoughts we are free to move into a new universe in which we experience the life of our dream.

Unconscious patterns, negative feelings, and beliefs often hold us back and we tend to repeat our worn out stories. In order to change, we need to dive into our subconscious and find a tunnel through time-space to transform our negative beliefs and patterns into positive ones.

You can find a positive potential hidden within any negative feeling. Anger wants to be heard, seen, un-derstood, and to create some kind of change. However, often despite our best attempts to transform our negative emotions, we tend to repeat the same behavior over and over again. Why is it that every New Year we make some more resolutions and weeks later we find ourselves repeating the same old pattern?

Many people give up because they don't know how to create the change.

During the seminar, I was getting a chance to demonstrate the power of this holographic transformation process. As far as a volunteer is concerned, I could not have asked for a better example. The woman who sheepishly raised her hand fit the picture of *not* living her potential. She was in her mid-forties, small, mousy and hardly visible. She spoke very softly and was living proof of low self-esteem. She was living in a lifeless and loveless marriage, not earning any money and wishing she was somewhere else. Her name was Martina.

I invited her to stand up and to close her eyes. In a gentle voice I asked Martina to think of her current reality and to feel how she was feeling when thinking about her current state.

We went through a series of questions aimed at feeling her current state of dissatisfaction. Getting in touch with the feelings of pain, anger and dissatisfaction does not have to be a drawn out long process. We can simply become aware of them long enough to start our transformation process.

Once she was in touch with her feelings I asked her to find the place in her body where she was feeling the sensations of her negative feelings the strongest.

She put her hands on her stomach because she felt the dissatisfaction as a gnawing feeling in her gut. She knew that she was staying in her current life situation for all the wrong reasons but she felt worthless and powerless to change any part. Placing security above her soul's expression and staying in a life of dependency was burdening her soul. She was aware of it through the feelings in her body. The body does not lie. You can fool your mind but you can't fool your body. Use your body as your own barometer. In time you will be highly capable of reading your body as if it was the most sensitive measuring device God ever created.

Once you locate the feeling in your body, you have already found the secret door to the new universe. We think we are living in a three dimensional world but really we are living in a sea of consciousness that expresses itself in an ocean of frequencies which in turn become the manifested world around you.

I asked Martina to notice the color, the shape and the form of this energy in her belly. Indeed, she could sense it. She could only see it vaguely at first but soon she was deeply in touch with her feelings and was able to see colors and shapes and had forgotten that we were all listening in.

I asked her to take this color and energy pattern outside of herself so we could take a look at it. In this state the colorful symbol functions like an independent being. Martina liked taking this feeling-energy-something outside of her body in order to look at it because it freed her of feeling the burden of the vacuum long enough to allow her to communicate with this energy-ball as an independent energy.

Embedded in the seemingly negative energy, we always find a truer, deeper, positive desire. Its needs may not be logical or even possible but all we need to know is WHAT IT REALLY WANTS. And low and behold when we asked it, this negative feeling took us to a parallel world and it showed Martina what it really wanted.

As though it had a mind of its own, it shared that it really wanted to live a happy and fulfilled life, one in which Martina was in love, living with passion and having a purpose. All negative feelings within us really wish to be empowered, radiant, strong and healthy. Our negative feelings are always just the flip side of the coin. Embedded in all negativity we find the positive intention. If we take time to listen to the negative feeling, it will always point us into the direction of where it (and thereby us) really wants to go.

With practice, you can use any of your negative feelings as a doorway to your deeper self and to the road of fulfillment. If you sit still and listen, your negative emotions will gladly tell you what they really want. Once you get access to your feelings, ask yourself: *"What do I really want to experience, or feel?"*

The negative energies can be easily located as feelings in our bodies, our heart, our belly, really anywhere. They can become our stepping stones to create what we really want.

The possibility of your fulfilled future exists right here and right now in the energy matrix of the time-space. Scientists are still trying to wrap their head around this issue. Let's use the metaphor of a parallel world in which the solution is interwoven within our reality but just a few notches away in vibration. To shift to a more fulfilled world, all we need to do is move our vibrational pattern up a notch and we will find ourselves in the space-time of our fulfillment.

Becoming aware of what we don't enjoy becomes the stepping stone and opens the door to the fulfilled solution. Instead of beating ourselves over the head for not doing or being what we want to do or be, we can use our shortcomings, our negative feelings to catapult us upward.

This story will show you the depth and breadth of what such a simple exercise can do.

We live in a living matrix of consciousness and we have discovered that we can literally shift time-space, if we treat life with the power of our awareness. Making this shift takes practice and the purification of our subconscious patterns, but we can all create great changes in our lives.

Standing in front of everyone, this mousy woman started to become aware of what she really wanted. I asked her to take an imaginary journey into the fulfillment. Noticeably to all of us, Martina started becoming aware of the feeling she would have, if her dream came true. Stepping into a new feeling, into a new energy matrix, is the first step to inform our energy body of the new and desired state.

Next I asked Martina to see what color the new energy would have, as well as what shape it would have and how it would feel in all of her cells, if this fulfilled feeling were present.

I guided Martina to thank the old energy for wanting

something so beautiful and we could all feel the deep sigh of relief as she let go inwardly. As she was honoring the old energy, it was willing to become the new fulfilled state. After all, that is what it had wanted all along.

Many well-meaning therapists ask their clients to eliminate, vaporize or otherwise eliminate the old energy. As if the negative energy could go away! We know from the law of preservation of energy that nothing ever gets lost!

Instead of getting rid of the old, we simply asked the old feeling-image if it was willing to become the new image. In essence the old image carries within it the seed of its own higher expression. Of course the old energy agreed because the old feeling of insecurity wanted nothing less than to feel strong.

These are just the general steps as the process goes a bit deeper. Next, we merged the old image with the new fulfilled image and voila, at the end of the session Martina stood there in front of the whole group with a radiant light and strength shining forth from her.

The miracle became evident to all of us the next morning. As we were just settling into our chairs, a new woman had walked into the seminar. I hadn't recognized her when she entered the room. Other participants in the group came up to me and pointed out this newcomer to me, alerting me to her presence. I went up to her and asked who she was. She laughed out loud! "I am the one you worked on yesterday morning, I was standing with you in front of the whole group!" she exclaimed.

WOW! Her visible transformation alone was a great proof for everyone in our seminar that this method was working miraculously.

However the real proof came the following year.

Martina joined us a year later in a repeat of the same seminar. As we all shared about ourselves, she told us about her journey of the last year. She had developed an Ideal-Self-image during the seminar a year ago. She had wanted to be an independent woman, strong, wealthy, radiant, and working in a way that she was passionate about.

Over the weeks and months following the seminar she entered her new feeling-images in her daily meditation. She was also following the *Living From Vision®* course and did the daily guided imagery exercises. One day she was told by her images to start *dressing up houses*. Martina had been building the power of her intuition and was able to listen to her inner nudges. She got the idea during one of her morning meditations to buy an older house, refurbish it, dress it up and re-sell it, fully decorated to new owners at a profit.

And that is what she did. It was a win-win situation for everyone because she used her talents, added value to the world around her and offered a service that others loved.

From the money she made, she went on to buy the next house. As the year came to an end, she was making her own income and had the power to separate from her husband. She had the trust, confidence and resources to step out on her own. And she felt glorious.

Martina had crafted herself into a higher version of herself like a stone carver would chisel out a masterpiece from a simple, rough rock.

Daily rehearsal of this new inner state brought about the kind of changes in her daily life that she could only dream of before.

How had it worked?

She had accessed her hidden feelings of inferiority, anguish, doubt and pain. Instead of ignoring her negative feelings, she brought them to light. Then she used the feelings and their underlying positive intention as a ladder to lead her to a new dimension in which she was feeling and living the way she really wanted to be. By focusing on how she really wanted to feel, she brought the potential that existed in a parallel dimension into the Here and Now. By connecting the old pattern with the new energy matrix, she honored the old pattern, gave it thanks and allowed it to become the new energy matrix. We built a bridge to Heaven.

In this case, Martina did the transformation via the anchor of a negative feeling. What you see around you and what is manifest around you, is in effect, a reflection of what you believe to be possible. Once you work on transforming the feelings that are in your way, bit by bit your subconscious and your aura will radiate the new YOU, until you are living the grander picture, the grander expression of yourself. By addressing and feeling into that which is currently holding you down, you will be able to morph into the fully radiant new YOU. By using the negative feelings, you can jump into your new matrix.

You don't need to have a problem or locate a negative feeling in order to move onward. You can set a positive goal intentionally or visualize a state you wish you embody and pre-experience it in advance. Imagine that somewhere you have a parallel YOU that is capable. And then start moving into that direction. Sooner or later you will walk into the new you. Call it your parallel "you" if you wish. In effect by imagining the other "you", you are setting up a *resonant field* which will help you draw that particular reality into this 3-D reality.

Whatever you experience now is in some way a reflection of an inner energy pattern that you hold in your auric field. The life-force duplicates your inner energy field into the outer reality. At any point in time you can choose to increase your vibrancy, and create a better life.

On that Saturday morning the previous year, Martina had made the first fundamental step to change her life. Every day thereafter she took time each day to merge into that new feeling-image. She reinforced the new energy matrix by using the daily morning and evening audio exercises with the *Living From Vision®* course.

The images started to guide her and she got new ideas from her daily inner dialog. She got a message one day, which told her "to dress up" a house. When she took that idea literally and followed it into reality, it became her ticket to success. Listening to our inner self speaking to us from a higher dimension will take us to our next level.

PROBLEMS AS STEPPING STONES

I had met Carol Wyn Williams during a seminar in Australia in 1999. She was excited to become an LFV Teacher and had her first goal set on looking better. Getting older had left its marks on her and she wanted to prove to herself that she could use her mind to create a change.

"Ilona," she wrote me after a few months of doing the LFV self-study course, "even my friends can hardly believe it, I look so young again." She had lost 28 pounds in a few months.

Here is the testimonial she wrote me to put on my website: "I can personally vouch for the change within me. Before staring the LFV course I had very little self-esteem and was overweight. As soon as I did the home study course, I started to change the way I thought of myself. I have lost 28 lb. since Christmas and I am now the size I was in my twenties (I'm 56 years old)."

I personally saw the proof when I met her about two years later. I was flying through Sydney and we met to discuss her successes teaching her LFV classes.

She told me an incredible story of a mom and her teenage son who was emotionally shut down and close to suicide.

The mom and the boy were not on great talking terms. Like many teenagers, he was mostly silent and withdrawn. At her wits' end, and trying to find some kind of bridge to her teenage boy, she suggested to him to take the LFV class in a group which Carol was teaching. He agreed and dragged himself to the class.

The first evening went well but the mom didn't have a chance to interact with her son during the classroom. She wondered if he was able and willing to follow the guided imagery exercises.

After the class they drove home and the mom turned to her son to ask him about his impression of the evening. Instead of being shut down he actually seemed interested in sharing. Soon they both started sharing about their experiences in the class, each sharing their own inner experiences. Intimacy often arises not from sharing about what we do, but rather what we feel inside. Sharing the inter-dimensional experiences brings people so much closer together in such a short amount of time that all couples should actually be required to learn how to do it.

They shared about how they each of them had imagined their own respective Place of Peace, and what kind of guide they had imagined.

When they arrived in the driveway, neither of them wanted to stop talking. In fact, Carol told me they shared and talked until 1 a.m., still sitting in the car.

The mom had called Carol in total excitement to share her magical experience she had had with her son! The conversation in the car was the first time in years that she had actually shared more than just a few seconds talking to her son.

During the course of the following weeks, the boy started glowing more and more each day. By the end of the fourth week, when the class content was about discovering ones life's purpose, he got a brilliant idea.

He wanted to start playing the piano again. It seemed like he had a genius talent hidden within him. Within a short amount of time his piano playing evolved into doing benefit concerts for children with cancer.

He wanted to utilize his burgeoning jazz piano skills to help those that had little time left on this Earth. In solidarity, he shaved his head. By offering benefit concerts and by helping others he made a come-back in his own life.

My jaw dropped as Carol told me the magical story of this mom and her teenage boy. The two of them had been amongst her first students!

Carol looked so fabulous herself. Gone was the grandmother look from the time when I first had met her. People who have read my book ***Dolphins, Love & Destiny*** might remember the first seminar in Australia when I went to see Merlin. Less than two years later, Merlin and I went through Sydney to visit Central Australia – to the Red Rock, Uluru.

On a stopover in Sydney, Carol met us at the airport. I had worn a bright orange outfit and a purple jacket and Carol came to greet me at the airport sporting a bright orange dress of the same color. It was as if higher synchronicities were at work. She looked stunning, probably 25 years younger. Her work on her inner psyche had paid off and she had proven to herself that she could set her goals with the *Living From Vision*® course and achieve them.

She loved looking younger and her self-esteem had grown, simply by diving into her inner world and focusing her attention on what she really wanted.

Not only was she growing and changing but now she was also helping others to grow and glow in the process. This method of changing ourselves for the better has a magnificent ripple effect into our world. One person at a time, we change ourselves and change others.

Using the very same technique, here is a remarkable a story about how an anorexic teenage girl was saved, minutes away from being force-fed through tubes in the hospital.

ANOREXIC GIRL COMES BACK TO LIFE

We all seem to have some kind of health issue afflict us or a loved one during our time here on Earth.

Not only do people suffer from having too much weight like Carol had in our previous story, there are those that have too little. Anorexia has many causes but here is a story of a girl that was able to heal from anorexia by transforming her inner emotional and mental landscape.

A naturopathic doctor had just participated in a seminar of mine in Germany, where she had studied the *Holographic Imaging Technique* (based on Dr. Vernon Woolf's work called *Holodynamics*). This is the imagery transformation technique that I described in the chapter about the woman who dressed up houses. If you have skipped through the book, it's definitely worthwhile reading the book from cover to cover but especially that chapter. The steps are also described in my children's book and app by the title of *"Alin Learns to Use His Imagination."*

I hadn't heard from this wild and enigmatic naturopathic doctor for over a year and then she came back to repeat one of our seminars. When she told the whole class the following story you could hear a pin drop in the room. Healing is a magical event for all of us here on this planet. Although it is only one of many things that our consciousness manifests, it is all the more important because it touches us at our root.

She told us that before attending the very first seminar about a year previously, some desperate parents had approached her as a last resort to help their anorexic girl. The girl was ready to be admitted to a clinic because she was losing weight so rapidly that the doctors feared for her life. As a matter of fact, they had decided to force-feed the girl to avoid damage to her organs.

Up until this point no therapy had helped and the parents as well as the doctors were at their wits' end. However, the idea of force-feeding their own daughter and seeing her plugged up with plastic tubes was revolting to the parents and, out of desperation, they went searching for alternative answers.

Nobody knew what had started the anorexia or how their daughter had gotten into this ghastly condition.

This naturopathic doctor had learned the Holographic Imaging Technique which we call Tracking, at my seminar just days after she had been asked by the desperate parents to intervene.

As soon as the doctor came home, she was eager to try the newly learned technique on this girl.

Since the girl had already been taken to the clinic, the naturopath asked to see the girl just a couple of times to try this new method before actually starting to force-feed her.

She asked the girl to close her eyes and to go to a place of peace. From there, she invited the full potential self of the girl to come to her. Then she gently talked the girl through the same questions I had shared earlier in a previous chapter.

Sure enough, there was darkness and heaviness which had settled into the girl's tummy. Undigested emotions, "unfinished business" as I call it, can usually be felt in one or another part of the body, usually associated with one of our energy centers, also called chakras.

She asked the girl when the energy/image had started and the girl suddenly recalled that it was when she befriended the girl from war-torn Serbia. This other young girl had not had enough to eat and was ghastly thin when they met.

It was a huge wake-up for both the doctor and the girl when they realized that this heavy energy that was residing in the anorexic girl's tummy was there as a feeling of solidarity with the Serbian girl.

Previously the anorexic girl had indeed had enough to eat, however the girl from Serbia hadn't had enough to eat. In psychology it is a known factor that people who survive calamities oftentimes feel guilty for the fact that they survive. Befriending this bereft girl from Serbia kicked in a sequence of thoughts and feelings that the subconscious mind of the girl was not equipped to handle.

Similar to survivors of calamities, this young girl had equally felt guilty for having it too good. In order to manage this level of guilt, instead of continuing living the life of luxury and having plenty of food, she had decided to join the ghastly thinness of the Serbian girl. This allowed her to be on equal footing.

This was the core reason why she had stopped eating and had become anorexic. If you look at it this way, there actually was a positive intention behind the apparent disease. Everyone could understand – the girl wanted to be in solidarity rather than in separation.

The first step had been made. The naturopathic doctor had found the positive intent behind the apparent negative energy. Out of solidarity, the girl had started to become anorexic. It was not even something the girl had chosen consciously.

Instead of suppressing or eliminating negative energies, she entered into dialogue with this inner apparent negative image and found the reason that had led to her anorexic condition. The inner images, which Dr. Woolf called *Holodynes* (holographical dynamically active energy-fields), are able to create change to our body functions and even create changes in our genes and our human actions. Furthermore, these images can even create changes at a distance, which Einstein called "Spooky Action at a Distance."

The girl was in a deeply relaxed state of daydreaming and the negative image was conveniently floating outside and in front of her. It is an important step to take, otherwise some very traumatic memories can shake the person up. When asking the image/energy that represents the original traumatic memory to reside outside of the body in order to be able to take a look at it, the emotions that the client experiences in relation to this dramatic event also become a lot less dramatic.

The next step to help bring about health was relatively easy. The naturopathic doctor asked this negative holodynamic image what it really wanted. As you already know, *what this feeling of solidarity really wanted was to be in solidarity.*

So the doctor asked the girl how it would be if both girls had a really vibrant and ecstatic friendship, in which they were both feeling this elated solidarity in a beautiful way. The girl instantly felt love and saw a wonderful light engulfing both of girls. In her image, both were radiant and in full health.

In one way, you might say that this answer was the polar opposite of what the girl had chosen. And yes that is true. That is often what we do. In order to solve a problem, we may resort to a rather primitive way of managing the problem. If you really communicate with any negativity, it will tell you that it has a deeper positive desire, which ultimately always wants to be expressed.

Research in this field has taught us that embedded within a negative spin is a positive spin. There is always a flip side to the coin.

The other side of a destructive negative wish is always a life-driven expression.

In thousands and thousands of hours of doing this work, we can say with 100% certainty there is always an embedded positive intention in anything negative.

When we take the time to listen to any negative feeling, we find out that it will reveal its truest wish, a positive expression of its own potential. Such is the nature of life. Out of compost grows another forest, a sunflower... life. The old expression then becomes absorbed and transformed into the new energy matrix.

What we need to do is ASK what it would feel like if it were already fulfilled. WHAT WOULD IT FEEL LIKE? That takes the tangent into its own future potential. That is how you bend time and space. That is how you do miracles. You allow everything to become its next expression of itself.

It will let you know. Just like the mousy woman in a previous chapter had transformed, just like the junk cars had disappeared suddenly or just like the check that came in the mail for Don, there is a positive potential hidden in every problem. Once we have a positive blueprint in our heart and mind, the universe will then listen, and respond. Our inner changes will express themselves in the real world, simply by shifting our inner fields and blueprint.

The deeper levels of the girl's subconscious and superconscious were able to deliver a healthier way of expressing solidarity with her friend from Serbia. Health, strength and true friendship are a lot more effective at sharing this solidarity and a lot more fun.

As soon as the session was done, the naturopathic doctor asked for two more days of not force-feeding the girl. "Just two days," she begged. She felt so confident that the girl had made a fundamental turnaround in her inner world, that the other doctors would surely see a change in the next two days.

And lo and behold, the girl started gaining her first 200 grams the very next day. Then the next day she gained another 200 grams, until she gained enough weight to be sent home.

One session of inner transformation had reset the balance in her inner world so much so, that the path she was on made a 180 degree turnaround.

When we learn how to navigate within time and space, we need to befriend the darkness and realize that it is part and parcel of the manifest world. The coin does have two sides, but we can hold the coin in our hand and not be afraid by what face is looking at us. The moment we communicate with the core essence of anything, it will transform into its next higher form of expression, into its next potential.

The negative problem is not in our way... it becomes the way, by becoming our stepping stone, which leads us to a fulfilled future.

It is great to have a therapist or doctor by our side, or even a friend who can walk us through such steps of transformation. But we don't always have a person by our side to guide us through such deep layers of our sub-conscious. Can positive focus alone help in our healing process?

HEALING THROUGH IMAGERY

FROM A WHEELCHAIR TO WALKING

Sometimes all it takes is time and persistence to see miracles come alive. Yes, when we want miracles we usually think of getting something manifesting instantly.

And what else is a miracle? Something happening that is truly out of the ordinary.

Let me tell you one of the most profound pieces of wisdom I learnt. It was from a 65-year-old man. He was the living proof that endurance and perseverance can create what will be a miracle.

Paul joined our one-week Dolphin Swim seminar in Florida, as I describe in my book *Wisdom of the Dolphins.*

He was fulfilling his life's dream. He was a vibrant 65-year-old man, jumping into the turquoise waters daily and frolicking with the dolphins. I marveled watching him jump into the waters and moving about like a young man. Not that many people at his age were that vibrant and alive.

I commented on this to Paul and the story he shared in response was so inspiring that I want to include it here in this book.

Paul had been tied to a wheelchair at age 50, when his doctor told him that he needed a spinal fusion, if he ever wanted to sort of walk again. If not, so he was told, he would be bound to his wheelchair for the rest of life.

182

Not taking no for an answer he refused to get a spinal fusion done and instead researched alternative healing. He had learned about the power of the mind, and he wanted some time to prove it to himself.

On a daily basis he started to drink a mixture of orange juice and agar-agar, a plant based gelatin, followed by sitting in silence and visualizing that this gelatin like mixture would feed the cushions between vertebrae of his lower spinal column. He imagined that these gelatinous discs were getting thicker and stronger with each passing day.

Slowly, ever so slowly, Paul noticed improvements, enough so, that he continued with his regiment. Not seeing instant transformation, nevertheless he felt that things were getting better.

He did this imaginary exercise every single day, day after day, month after month, year after year until he got the results he wanted. After 4 long years Paul was able to walk again, and decided he was good enough to see his doctor again. As Paul walked into the office and asked to be given an X-ray the doctor looked at him in disbelief. He gave him the X-ray and then, befuddled, held up the old X-rays. "That can't be you," the doctor retorted. "You must be his brother, and are trying to trick me."

The doctor could not believe it. But here was the evidence – a real X-ray – living proof before his very own eyes.

Paul continued his regiment for another four years with his daily visualization method and agar-agar because his goal was not just to be able to walk, but also to be 100% pain-free.

At the end of those eight years, Paul indeed was pain-free and walking, much to the shock of his doctor.

Here we were swimming with dolphins and I witnessed him jumping around on our boat like a young man.

Since his own healing, Paul took it upon himself to teach spinal recovery through the use of the imagination and agar-agar to another fifty people by the time I had met him.

This was not an isolated feat that one blessed man was able to do. Instead, it is repeatable, and fifty others that Paul taught personally, have followed his example.

If one of us can do it, we all can. At times, all we need to know is that others have succeeded before us.

Do you recall the famous verse by Jesus (John 14:12): Whoever believes (in me) will also do the works and even greater things than these!

We can succeed in creating miracles. They are simply miracles because they are out of the ordinary. Some beings who have enough belief in a higher force, or who are awake enough to realize the nature of the matrix, and the ONENESS of all life, can create something that other people cannot. They have realized that life is much greater than what meets the eye. A greater force is at work. A universe that is listening.

What these stories do, is give us the faith, trust, or the willingness to explore and to start communicating with that greater force. "God", "The Universe", call it what you wish.

Dream Big – THE UNIVERSE IS LISTENING.

Times have changed, and more people are now partaking in these mystery teachings than ever before. I hope you're taking full advantage of this opportunity. You've been given the gift to be able to read, we've been given the gift to be able to share the stories out in the open, for everyone to see who has ears to listen.

Currently we're entering the time when quantum thinking will become commonplace. We are slowly updating the way we think about the universe. Our perception of what reality actually is, is different now compared to what it was a few thousand years ago. There is something afoot that science has yet to comprehend. We live in a Consciousness Interactive Universe. The faster you vibrate, the faster the results.

At times the changes come miraculously fast, at times, like in this story, the miracle required perseverance. But the miracles come about. Whatever you ask for from this universe, with all sincerity, will come about sooner or later.

Let's take a look at our DNA and the field of epigenetics. Even science is starting to agree with us here.

ACTIVATING YOUR DNA

More and more evidence is coming out that shows that our DNA is not only a book of set instructions but that we are equally writing and re-directing and igniting certain aspects of our DNA depending on the environment. "Epigenetics" has become a mainstream word.

Epigenetics has been used to describe altered genetic expression, when the DNA was set to do something otherwise. It is now understood that our environment causes the turning on and turning off of certain genetic factors. **Bruce Lipton** has been a trendsetter in this field with his book ***The Biology of Belief***.

We might be born with a particular tendency but depending on the lifestyle we lead, the food we eat, the thoughts we think and the air we breathe, different genes within our DNA will get activated.

But not only our environment changes how our DNA responds, but also – and here comes the most exciting news – our attitudes affect our gene expression. An experiment done by Glen Rein showed how a DNA strand that was observed under the microscope would change its form depending on whether it was exposed to feelings of anger or love. It was positioned next to a person who was directed to go through a variety of emotions. The DNA coil contracted when exposed to fear and the same DNA strand expanded its coil when it was exposed to love.

When we are contracted and feel confusion and fear, we lose all insight, all connection to the higher force.

186

But when we are open, when we are radiantly feeling love, our DNA become an expanded antennae and is able to transduce more information from a higher dimension into our system. Our DNA functions more like an antenna to gather information from a higher level. The coding is apparently not etched permanently into stone, nor is the DNA apparently a solid book of instructions. The DNA seems to be able to be changed! It is already well known that it can change according to the environment it is in.

For example: In a rat study, rats with DNA predisposed to grow cancerous tumors did not do so if the rat was fed a particular nutrient. Interestingly, thoughts and emotions do the same as nutrients.

Don and I have found out that seeds, for example, can be grown to ten times their sprouting size when sent "good" information alone. Remember my information about the SE-5 and all the research being done in Europe, Mexico, China, and North America?

Our western scientists are now beginning to acknowl-edge that our DNA may connect our cellular body to a *higher bandwidth of frequencies.*

The environment you live in and what you eat is only part of what changes your DNA. Your thoughts and emotions do so as well. What you are able to tune into, the "radio station" you have your DNA tuned to, will determine the outcome as well.

An LFV teacher in Germany wanted to prove to herself that she could also use the imagination to change her physical state of health. She started to imagine that her warts were melting away. She had had warts on her hands and feet since her teenage years. Low and behold, after just a few weeks of her focusing on her health in this way, the warts were gone! She simply imagined the end result that she wished to have. She didn't imagine eliminating the warts with negative thoughts, negative imagery or any kind of elimination technique. She simply imagined the end result of what she wanted – healthy skin.

In other words she didn't spend her time thinking about how she would get to her desired goal. She simply spent time in BEING in the state of her desired end result.

When you set up a resident holographic field around yourself by occupying the future in advance or the final emotional state that you will experience once you arrive at your destination, you create the field that then finds its matching physical expression.

The universe needs you to set up such a resonant field.

Unfortunately many people stare at the problem and worry about it getting worse instead of better. Instead, we need to REFOCUS on what we want and make REFO-CUSING a POSITIVE HABIT.

Refocusing on what we really want doesn't imply not looking at what is.

In fact, we need to deal with what is at hand and fully realize where we really want to be. If we realize that all difficulties become our stepping stones into a fulfilled future, from now on we will embrace any challenge, communicate with it, and find out where it came from.

Challenges simply point out where some energy has gotten stuck, where there is some unfinished business and what still needs to be purified in us in order for us to become a more brilliant, greater diamond of light manifest.

By providing a positive state and imagining a fulfilled result, our emotional body will supply the universe with a blueprint of what to create.

Since I had heard the story about this woman healing her warts, I wanted to try it myself. I tried a similar method for myself but the healing came in a different form. I call it a secondary method.

For a few minutes here and there, I focused my mind and visualized the outcome of the wart being gone. I felt happy with my healed skin and felt grateful.

Before too long, I found myself standing in the checkout stand in a health-food store one day. I overheard a conversation where one person was telling another person about the fact that just a drop of *Grapefruit Seed Extract* applied onto a wart just a few times during one month was enough to make a wart disappear.

I immediately got some grapefruit seed extract and applied it just like she had said, a couple of times during a month onto my skin. My wart went away! My end result was the same; I had healthy skin. Was it my mind or my imagination that healed my body? I certainly had created the blueprint for my healed condition in my own inner mind and heart. By creating the final end result of my healed skin, I had set a field into motion which brought the healing into my life. The appropriate and needed information found its way into my field quickly because I had set up an end result that I desired.

I learned that our imagination will bring about the results which we look for, in a way that is harmonious with our beliefs. I drew an answer toward me that would help me achieve my desired result. The LFV teacher in Germany had used her mind alone because that's what she wanted to prove to herself. She wanted to achieve the result with only her imagination. As she created an internal blueprint with the belief that she could do it, her body followed suit.

Healing can come in many wondrous ways. It is our job to invent the future and the future will unfold in accordance with our beliefs. The more you practice and the more you realize that you do live in a dreaming universe, the more you will allow yourself to achieve whatever it is you want.

The laws by which the universe is operating grow with you as you grow. Change yourself in order to allow for more and more miraculous manifestation. Looking from the inside out, these changes will simply feel natural because they only happen when you feel that they should.

You will find support for your imagined future when you focus towards the higher dimensions and ask for support. There is a force field, let's call it God, that is greater than yourself and will support you in miraculous ways.

To demonstrate how the power of the higher dimensions come to our aid, let me tell you this next story:

A woman that I had interviewed for the DREAM BIG ONLINE SUMMIT, by the name of Paivi, had been diagnosed with leukemia at the age of eighteen months.

Nothing the doctors did worked or helped.

The little girl's parents were deeply religious and lived in a very religious community. The community held vigils and prayer circles yet nothing had helped so far.

The doctors called the mom and told her that the daughter was going to die within the next 24 hours and asked her to arrange things for that dreadful outcome.

But instead of taking the verdict, this woman listened closely to the inner voice of divine inspiration in her heart. When this inner voice told her to go pick up her daughter NOW she convinced her husband to snatch the baby out of the hospital unbeknownst to the doctors and bring her home.

She excused herself to the doctors later on by telling them that if her daughter was going to die she might as well die at home.

But this little voice inside her heart, which felt like divine guidance, had told her in no uncertain terms, that if she *picked up the baby now,* it would live.

The father was currently a taxi driver, and they snuck into the morning shift at the hospital the following day. Nobody noticed that they had taken the baby out of the hospital wrapped up in white sheets. The doctors were shocked, however miracles over miracles, the baby lived.

Now as an adult woman in her mature years she is a living witness to a miraculous healing.

Vigils had been held, as well as prayer circles and blessings had been made and collective requests for the baby to live had been sent to the universe.

When it looked like nothing was helping, listening to that still voice within the mother's heart was what made the big difference.

Paivi told me how her parents and the community held a strong belief in miracles which created the blueprint for the healing. They asked for a miraculous healing. They reached their hand into the heavens.

But then there was timing. When the mother was told to get her daughter out of the hospital right then and there, she followed. And because she listened, she witnessed the miracle manifesting right in front of her eyes. Within 24 hours the girl was healed.

The universe was reaching the other proverbial hand down to Paivi, communicating to her and telling her to do something at a particular time.

We need to develop the skills to listen to the guidance from the inner world, from God, or whatever you wish to call it. We need to practice listening.

Voices can come from all directions. We have to learn to decipher which ones come from a higher dimension, which ones to follow. That ability only comes with time. We need to train ourselves daily by listening to inner silence.

When we reach out into the higher dimensions to ask for a dream to be fulfilled, be it health, relationships, strength, or a creative project, we need to do our part. The universe will then reply and the fuel for the manifestation comes from a higher dimension.

Soon we slowly realize that we live in a co-creative field that makes dreams and miracles possible.

THE WHOLE AND ITS PARTS

In this next story that I am about to tell you, I will share how I worked at stretching my own boundaries of beliefs. It is very magical and I have it on video.

You see, it is not a question if manifestation works or even how it works. A large part of why I'm sharing these stories is to help you *build your belief* that *you can create your world with your consciousness and focus.*

The stories that I am sharing in this book can help us see the world through different eyes. It is in partly the depth or strength of our belief that shifts reality. In the end, it is really not a question as to whether manifestation can work or not.

The real question we have to deal with has to do with what we personally believe is possible. These beliefs can be embedded deeply into our subconscious mind. This is a very, very subtle issue. We have beliefs that reach deep into our subconscious and reach high up into the invisible worlds, into the ultra- dimensional worlds that are beyond our conscious grasp.

It is the very beliefs which we hold in the crevices of our conscious, subconscious and superconscious mind that have determined the BOUNDARIES by which we live.

In other words, that which we believe will determine what we can and cannot do.

Everything has a boundary. So let's make friends with

it. Boundaries are wonderful. They allow you to be you and me to be me. They allow us to interact. They also allow us to co-create something new and creativity to blossom. They also help us to look back at the very same source from whence we came and to realize the oneness within it. Boundaries allow the oneness to experience itself looking back at itself. In this loop of the "creator" and the "created" meeting itself, an immense ecstasy is released. If you've ever felt the direct gaze of God upon you in your meditations or prayer, you know what I'm talking about.

Boundaries really are very beautiful things. Boundaries allow reality as we know it to exist. They allow one thing to be differentiated from something else. They allow individuality. The downside of boundaries is that we have to experience and accept the opposites.

Opposites are sometimes hard to accept because they are so *"other than ourselves."* But without boundaries, there would be no creation and no perception of creation.

This individuation of creation allows perception of something. The most beautiful love affair arises when the created and the creator dance in union, if I may be a little poetic.

Manifestation has many levels. It is an ever ascending spiral that reaches into higher and higher octaves.

Whatever level we are currently at appears stable to us.

Anything vibrating higher than ourselves will appear as invisible and slightly out of reach. Anything vibrating slower than ourselves will appear as lower, denser and usually therefore less attractive.

If you raise your vibration to an even higher level, you start embracing time-space at greater and greater intervals. Once you reach the ability to embrace the entirety, then you can become the Alpha and the Omega. You start living with eternity at your core.

From that level of awareness you will experience so much compassion for all of creation and you will be understanding and be naturally patient. Learning about manifesting a better life leads you along the staircase of a natural evolution of consciousness. As you move through the levels of increased understanding of reality you will be able to experience greater love, compassion, bliss, ecstasy and you will be able to live in fulfillment.

Whatever appears as a solid reality is in fact interactive consciousness. Miracles cannot exist as an anomaly in nature. A fluke. A mistake. No, they are the harbinger of what is to come in our future evolution of mankind. The more you raise your awareness level, the more you live in beauty. Your wishes manifest in accordance with your ability, clarity, and strength that you develop on this journey called life.

So when you wish to alter the universe you live in, you actually have to work on elevating your state of consciousness. To the degree that you are able to focus your attention, energy and create coherence within your own energy body, to that degree you can manifest things at will.

Of course the speed at which you manifest things has to do with your own self-imposed limiting beliefs.

FLOWER MANIFESTATION

Trying to be like a Yogi

I was about to give a lecture at the Prophet's Conference in the USA with approximately 700 + people in the audience. Most people in the audience were savvy and accustomed to hearing about the subject of higher consciousness. I was in the company of other lecturers like Barbara Marx Hubbard, the late astronaut Edgar Mitchell, Gregg Braden, Jean Houston and the late Huston Smith, all of whom I adore.

I sat in my hotel room before coming down to the lecture hall and closed my eyes. I wanted to do an experiment that day. My lecture was about the power of our consciousness. Naturally when talking about something, it is also a really good idea to be a master of it.

Since I was going to speak about co-creation and the effects of consciousness on time-space and matter, I wanted to demonstrate something that I had never done before. Jokingly in the past, I had told people to watch my hands as I was about to manifest an orange in my hand. But truthfully I never once thought that could happen.

When I wondered about it, I realized that I didn't even eat oranges, so I most likely would not have any real need to manifest any. When I did try to manifest one, someone usually brought me an orange within the hour.

I had heard about instant manifestation. And as you have read, I had seen some with my very own eyes. Yet

197

I had never created something which I consider a deep yogic achievement; for example creating a flower in the hand instantly.

Maybe you have heard about such feats already. Yogis and other masters, foremost in the Far East, have created flowers, ashes or even jewels right there on the spot.

I had various successes in other areas and today I wanted to try to do something that went far beyond what I had done so far in my life.

In the past, one of the reasons why I was hesitant to create something out of thin air, or so I reasoned, was the possibility of people falling to my feet. I did not want people following me like a saintly guru.

If you were a person who could manifest something in your hand out of thin air, let's say a flower or diamond, what would your friends or your family members think? How would others you work with treat you?

Do please take a moment to think about this with me.

What would you think and feel?

I had gone to India and watched such live performances. I had watched them on video close up and zoomed in.

Discovering our comfort zone about manifesting something is an important step in making progress in manifesting something that we want. When I first thought about it in a small group of magical friends, we all agreed that 24 hours was fast enough for us.

Others may be more comfortable to have something manifest in a day, others in a week, a month, or maybe even years. It is up to us what we can handle and most of all what we can accept.

The day I was to present to over 700 people the lecture about the nature of consciousness and how it interacts with matter, I wanted to overcome my hesitance to manifest something instantly in front of people.

As I sat in meditation, I started to imagine a flower appearing in my hand, right in front of the audience. I held this image and feeling of allowing this kind of miracle to happen during my lecture, until I was able to fully believe it with all my heart and bones.

You know when something resonates into our bones that it is true. That is the feeling I was waiting for. I felt this certainty running up and down my spine. Each of us has a different barometer. You need to discover yours. When all your cells say YES, this is the way it is; it is so.

When I felt this certainty, I went downstairs to the hall just in time to listen to Cody Johnson make his beautiful announcement of my name and giving a short introduction.

It was time for me to walk up on stage. Glaring lights were blindingly shining into my eyes, which was comforting as I didn't really see the large audience.

I started out by playing some Native American flute. At one point I said "If we could just get out of our local time thinking and into quantum thinking, the kinds of miracles we could have are instantaneous transformation UsuallyI do it like this...I am practicing right now".

Much like a stage magician does before manifesting something, but without saying "*abracadabra*" I went once around in a circle with my hand and on the second time around, voila I suddenly had a Hawaiian Ginger flower in my hand.

I stared at the Hawaiian Ginger flower perched between the fingers of my left hand, I was holding a flower out to the audience. I nearly jumped out of my skin. What had happened?

I said on camera: "I am better than I thought!" and all of us were laughing.

But what had really happened? My mind reeled. I had swung my left arm in a large hocus-pocus type movement to my left making a large circle and then suddenly I held the flower in my hand. Yes, I had wanted that. But in all honesty, although I had prepared myself for this, I also didn't quite believe it. It came as a bit of a shock.

In a flash I figured it out and my left brain was happy again. Remember the logical mind does not like to have things be too far out of the norm.

Here is the answer:

Inadvertently, during this circling of my arm in the attempt to create a sudden appearance of a flower in my hand, my physical hand had in some mysterious way gotten hooked into the flower arrangement, which was behind me to my left. There stood a beautifully decorated vase of huge Hawaiian flowers.

Although I had not consciously seen this vase and the flowers, my greater awareness must have seen it. Or so I reasoned now. There must be a logical explanation!

Indeed, a flower had appeared in my hand but that was

too much for me to handle. A reasonable explanation was that my fingers of my left hand had gotten tangled in the flower arrangement behind me and I had effortlessly pulled a flower out of the large vase during my hocus-pocus movements.

Instantly my left brain was satisfied to have found a logical explanation and I pointed the probable cause of how this miracle had happened out to the whole audience.

What is important for us to note here is this: I did create what I had set out to do and yet I created it in accordance with what I was comfortable with.

When I did have the flower in my hand, just like I had imagined, I was still shocked. I needed a good explanation. And so I got what I wanted. There was a good explanation that allowed me to remain a normal mortal.

Similar to the story of landing in Washington DC, instead of being re-routed to Baltimore as was planned, I had felt that same certainty in my spine today.

But today I was doing this experiment in front of an audience. Deep down inside I really didn't want to be too different from the rest of humanity. I created this miracle in a way that allowed me to look like everyone else.

Everyone laughed and maybe some people thought that I must have rehearsed this move really well.

The fact is that I had not rehearsed it. I didn't even know that there were flowers behind me. I was too busy walking on stage, seeing the glaring lights and getting ready to play my flute.

And yet I manifested the flower in my hand just like I had envisioned, in perfect keeping with my beliefs, wants and fears. Limits and all, I got what I was able to handle. No more, no less.

I had been willing to stretch my beliefs a little bit, and therefore the desired results did happened. But this manifestation was still in alignment with my deeper beliefs and fears.

Like I said earlier, when Don and I first studied with Dr. Vernon Woolf and deeply realized that we are living in a quantum state of flux all of the time and that life is much like a hologram, we gathered with our co-students and discussed an important question: HOW FAST COULD WE HANDLE CHANGE?

We discussed the speed of manifesting that we were willing to accept or shall I say, that we were able to handle.

We took this question seriously, and I want to ask you the same question.

This question allows you to discover which underlying beliefs you hold about shifting realties. Find out what beliefs constitute your boundaries.

I like the metaphor that we live in a sea of quantum foam which is "there" 50 billion times per second and which is "gone" 50 billion times a second.

This undulating quantum foam allows us to shift in between time-lines and choose harmonious, loving worlds any time we wish.

We might think that there is a world out there, but it is

all just a mirage, like the Rishis of old have said. As long as we vibrate at the same rate as our surroundings, then the reality around us seems solid. But when we vibrate at a higher rate, even slightly higher or finer you might say, then time-space arranges itself a little faster in accordance with our thoughts, feelings, beliefs and our openness to the higher source.

Let me tell you about some daily miracles from our many adventures Rishikesh, India.

DAILY MIRACLE STORIES

FROM RISHIKESH

Here are a few short stories that happened in Rishikesh, India since we started on our trail to the Far East. Each story demonstrates how our inner dimensions and our focus influences our daily reality.

I realize that some readers, maybe you, have been working in this field for a long time. There may be tidbits in the next few pages that can reignite something in you. For other readers, some points will be the beginning of a journey of discovery to a greater life. Whichever it is, let yourself be inspired.

Some of the unfolding stories in this book will be outlandish, so much so, that they can be hard to believe. However, they happened as I wrote them. I make it a point to only write what is true. As I share the stories, I will share steps along the way that you can take to make miracles come true in your life.

Very likely you have experienced coincidences in your life. There are times when you think of someone and they call you. You pray for a parking spot and there it is, in the perfect place, at the perfect time. Many readers who have read some of the other miracle stories in my previous books have been inspired. When faced with similar challenges, they took the steps that I had described and created equally powerful outcomes in their own lives.

Sometimes we just need to be reminded to DREAM BIG

and ask for miracles. Many times we just need dare to imagine our bigger self, our much more radiant self. All too often we slip into mediocracy and need to jolt ourselves out of the hypnotic state of acceptance of what the norm is on our planet.

Remembering who we are and what we can be is a lifelong endeavor. As humans, we can have the tendency to get caught up in our daily routines and we need to lift our sight above the clouds. We can actually reinvent ourselves every day.

We might write miracles off to inexplicable coincidences and might want to push them aside as a nice surprise. But if you start taking note of them, they will multiply, just like a well-tended garden which will then bear more and more fruit. You can start to expect miracles daily and find that these miracles build your confidence.

I had been practicing my daily morning and evening meditation for decades since my teenage years. The daily guided morning and evening meditations from the *Living From Vision®* course have been especially helpful. I still do them pretty much daily.

THE MONKEY MIND

Let me fast forward twenty years from our first trip to India. Don and I had discovered Rishikesh on one of our many visits to India since our Japanese author and organizer had taken us to see the gurus and babas.

We had just arrived in Rishikesh, the place where the Beatles had discovered Maharishi, and we decided to spend one month here to recuperate and me to write my book.

Don and I were staying at a hotel with a perched view of the Ganges River which was raging straight down from the Himalayas. Every morning Don and I went down to the banks of the Ganges River to sit on one of the big rocks in the brilliant sunshine during the early February crisp air to meditate.

The sun shone straight into my third eye as I faced the water. I was basking in so much light and loved the feeling that we had all the time in the world to ourselves. I was in bliss. One month of no demands on me or us, other than to meditate and to write. We had left our 30+ employees in Bali to take care of our *Shambala Retreat Center* and enjoyed being able to focus on our inner life.

But as you may know from your own meditations, thoughts have a tendency to creep into our silent mind.

At the beginning of unguided meditation, many thoughts can arise, especially if one has not kept house, so to speak, for a while. It is often referred to as the monkey mind and this usually dissuades many people from going further in their meditations. They say that they are not good at meditating and give up.

Today it was the same for me. Thoughts kept jumping around my mind. "Unfinished business" I call it. My daily diary was sitting next to me, containing the record of my *To Do Lists* and insights. I wrote down my many thoughts as reminders of what to do when I came back to work. Writing those jumpy thoughts down, right at the beginning of a meditation phase, for just 10 minutes can give you great peace, without effort.

Running a Retreat Center like we do in Bali is a great

blessing, but it also requires time and attention to the many little things. While sitting there on the rock on the banks of the glorious Ganges River that day, I remembered that I had not answered a particular group leader who had written to us urgently needing an answer. My assistant was not able to give the answer and so I needed to help out.

I wrote this memory down and blessed this thought as it came to my awareness. Blessing our thoughts or worries, and letting them be taken into an imaginary river of light, aka the Hands of God, is akin to asking the larger super computer to come up with a good solution. We can let the grander wisdom of the universe handle our issues. Blessing our thoughts and worries is my way of asking for help from the unseen worlds. How well that works can be seen in this little story that evolved.

Sitting at the foothills of the Himalayas and in the valley of the river, I could feel the immensity of the many yogis who had gone before me here on the banks of the Ganges River into the realms of enlightenment. The whole valley was filled with the imprints of the many yogis who had gone before me, then and now. What a blessing it was to be here in this misty glow of enlightenment. Basking in the glorious sunshine, a silly thought arose in my mind's eye. The group leader with the issue came to my mind.

"How about a yummy cake and some chai?" Don said to me after we came out of our meditation. "Yes!" I chimed in and up we climbed the many stairs back up to our hotel. Adjacent to our Divine Resort Hotel was the Divine Cafe. If offered an appealing array of European looking cakes on display.

Chocolate German Cake, and Blueberry Cheesecake had my attention. As you might recall, I didn't eat any sweets for about 20 years of my life as a spiritual practice until the day that I saw the movie "Au Chocolat!" where the pious priest wound up laying on a bed of chocolate and cakes after he had gorged himself on the sins of life.

I have since decided that moderation is the answer, so today I looked at all the many chocolate cake options.

"Aren't you Ilona?" a woman's voice asked me from the right side. She had also been gazing at the same cakes. A gorgeous young woman with an accent seemed to know me. I looked at her in astonishment. I was bewildered that someone recognized me here in India far away from the circles of my friends. I looked at her and slowly realized that it was the woman from my meditation! This was the group leader who had wanted to come to stay at our *Shambala Retreat Center* in Bali and had requested something that my assistant had not been able to answer.

"Oh my God!" I exclaimed. "I was seeing you in my inner mind in my meditation today and really wanted to talk to you!"

It seemed like she had literally manifested out of thin air for me to deliver the message to her personally. The last time we had seen each other had been in Bali a few months ago. All three of us sat down to share some chai and cake and we arranged all the details that she needed to know in order to make her decision. What was odd was that although Rishikesh and Laxman Julah, where we stayed, was not a very large area, we never saw each other again in the weeks to follow. It was the only time I saw her during my one month's stay in Rishikesh.

Did blessing my monkey mind thoughts that morning during my meditation, and turning the unfinished business over to the greater power of the universe have this miraculous effect of arranging our meeting?

THE SAINTLY SADHU BEGGAR

A few weeks later, just a few days before Don was about to fly to a meeting in Mumbai, we meandered through the dusty roads of Laxman Julah. We walked along the many colorful shops which were offering the most magnificently embroidered blankets and bags and even embroidered shoes. Cows grazed through the rubbish on the side of the road and someone was feeding a cow with precious bread. The cows in India are holy and not to be eaten. Hence there were a lot of them at times standing in the middle of the road, undeterred by the noisy honking of the taxis, trucks and rickshaws that all competed for space. India is indeed noisy and often crowded, but it is so wild and wondrous and you find pilgrims and offerings wherever you look. Passing by a very colorful ashram, the gatekeepers were begging us to enter. Flowers, flower petals and flower wreaths were sold in the many stalls by the roadside as offerings. Smoke arose everywhere from perfumed incense and wherever I looked, Indian and western pilgrims lined the streets.

On our path down to the ashram where Prem Baba was giving his satsangs, I had met this one particular Krishna Sadhu. Like a beggar, he always sat by the side of the steps right by the curve where the steps merge into the road that comes down from the upper road leading to the Ganges. Amidst the many little shops, beggars, and shop keepers, he stood out like a blazing light. His eyes were brilliant, serene and always met mine in a deep gaze whenever I passed him by. And each time I passed him by, I gave him a good amount of money. But because I had been writing a lot, I had not gone down into town that often and was starting to miss seeing him. I also reasoned that he must be missing me.

One problem was that right next to him sat at least one if not two more begging sadhus that eagerly wanted to get some money as well. To make matters worse, they usually got coins and/or small bills rather than what I wanted to give my saintly beggar who always got quite a bit more than was usual.

Today as I walked past some of the shops I got this brilliant idea to stop and get out the appropriate bills so that when I was ready to give him his alms, no one had to see how much it really was. Envy seemed to exist even amongst these sadhus.

I got out my 500 rupiah bill out, about 10 USD worth and was thinking about running down to where my favorite sadhu usually sat. We were still up the road a bit and I wanted to make sure I met my saint today.

Just as I turned to tell Don that I wanted to take the money over to him, this very saintly sadhu appeared right next to me. Startled, I shook from having him soundlessly appear virtually one foot away from me. He never ever left his post except to go home at 5 p.m. every day. Now he was standing next to me, quite a bit away from his usual spot.

He was equally taken by the coincidence as I turned

to him. Quickly I put the 500 rupiah bill into his hands and told him it was for him. He probably had no idea that I had literally just taken the money out of my wallet to take it over to him. The timing was perfect. I did not have to deal with all the other beggars and he and I could give each other a deep hug. He was literally appearing just the moment I was ready.

This moment was timed to perfection, showing me that when we are in tune, as regular meditation does for us, all things can literally appear at the right time in the right place for us, especially if that is your inner prayer or mantra.

THE LOTUS FLOWER

The week before, I had passed a perfectly blossoming lotus flower. The light of the afternoon sun lit the yellow stem inside the pink lotus flower and radiated with a supernatural light. I was in a bit of a hurry and needed to get to my massage appointment. But loudly and clearly my inner voice said "Stop now, and take a picture!" I was under pressure to be on time and really questioned the need to take this picture. I ever so lightly hesitated, but then luckily, since I have gotten used to listen to my inner voice, I did stop and quickly got my cell phone out and placed it to take the picture.

A lotus flower that is perfectly open and translucently lit is a wonderful blessing to behold. We don't see one every day. The miracle and the lesson happened as I took my first photo. Just as I clicked to take the photo, one of the petals fell off and in its place was a gapping space.

In the photo that I actually took, due to the ever so

small delay and hesitation on my part, shows the small gap. But it got better. The breeze that had taken out the one petal, started to take out one petal after another as I still tried to take more and more photos. In a matter of less than thirty seconds the fully opened lotus flower lost her petals. Had I hesitated more than a split second to take the picture, I would not have gotten the truly magical image of the lotus flower. I posted it on Instagram and it looks like one of those award-winning photographs.

One second longer or if I had waited until after my massage, the entire flower would have been gone. Such is life. Perfectly timed. We are not just walking through time and space. There are different realities awaiting us at different nodule points in different times and spaces. One moment longer, where we don't listen to our inner nudge, and we are out of the perfect alignment.

Conversely if we listen to the inner voice, the one that my mom tried to teach me to listen to so early on in my life, we are in the perfect time at the perfect place. This next story is a perfect example of such divine timing.

RAMANA's GARDEN – THE UNTOUCHABLES DREAM

"Why, why are these precious children called The Untouchables? How can I help in this misery?"

Deva's heart was sobbing. She had been living in a cave on the banks of the Ganges River, pursuing her enlightenment because her guru had told her to seek the wisdom of the Mother of all Rivers called the Ganges.

While living in her cave, seeking to find her own enlightenment, she had witnessed on a daily basis these so-called "untouchables" in India. They were forced to live close to the banks of the rivers in tents, trying to eke out their survival in the foul smelling trash of other humans. Watching the untouchables broke her heart. These children were never allowed to enter a school, never allowed to open a bank account, and never were given adequate health care. But instead of giving in to the agony of seeing the lives of the untouchables and surrendering to what is the norm in India, Deva wowed to make a difference. She now had a BIG DREAM: She wanted to make a difference to these people.

Eleven clinics, building schools upon schools, she started to do the unimaginable. Where there was no way, she created a way.

What do Saints do, you may ask? Do they also still have dreams? Do they still create? Do they have visions and desires?

Instead of fulfilling her own needs, she focused on creating a better world for others. The words *Living Her Life's Purpose* had achieved a higher meaning. Not just pondering the meaning of her own life, she like other saints started to gain meaning by helping others. Deva Dwabha created Ramana's Garden which is an amazing orphanage at the banks of the Holy River, the mother of all rivers, the Holy Ganges. It is an orphanage of children who come from a different world. Denied to have dreams, she gave the children the vision that all things are possible and the hope for a better life.

Deva Dwabha really started having dreams and wishes. Whereas previously she had lived a life of fulfilling desires of glamour and money, renown and glitz, her desires had now gained a new dimension.

Ramana's Garden was named after the renowned Advaita Teacher Ramana Maharshi, whose image I always have on my altars. This orphanage, school and restaurant offers vegetarian food to the public and to the conscious visitor. The funds that she derives from the restaurant feed the children, clothe them and offer these outcast children schooling.

Dwabha (for short) had come to India about 34 years prior, following the teachings of Osho. Later another guru sent her to live at the banks of the Ganges telling her that the river would teach her about enlightenment. Living in a cave like a proverbial yogini, she had to witness so much suffering by watching her neighbors, the garbage pickers, who also lived at the river's banks.

It was through a twist and turn of events that opened her heart to such a degree that she found the path to enlightenment via her service to humans who were much more in need than her.

Ramana's Garden had come recommended to me by our friend Margot Anand, an international author and, you may know, brought tantra to the West. She has written numerous books including *The Art of Sexual Ecstasy; The Art of Everyday Ecstasy*; and *The Art of Sexual Magic.*

Margot Anand and Deva Dwabha had spent time at Osho's commune together. Deva and her work with the orphans at Ramana's Garden came highly recommended by Margot and I was told by her not to miss it. Dwabha was a sort of Mother Theresa, as I found out.

Later she allowed me to bring my Hindi version of my book *Alin Learns to Use His Imagination* in the form of an app to the children. It is called RAVI.

Dwabha's lifelong motto had been to dream, to know that having dreams can create a better life, and she welcomed my children's book and the techniques which it teaches. I had the book translated into Hindi and had just created an app of the book so that it functioned like an e-book which also included four guided meditations, all recorded in Hindi.

Embedded in the fairytale of the children's book are amazing transformation tools, which are based on the teachings of Dr. Vernon Woolf and his work called Holodynamics. I had been teaching that technique for the last twenty-five years mostly to therapists, teachers and healers worldwide and have written about the technique in my other books.

The children read the book in the form of an app on the donated Androids which they had been fortunate enough to receive from another donor.

They listened to the Hindi guided imagery exercises with full attention (later I produced the same app in English) and started drawing pictures in the app from their experiences that they had during their meditations.

It was amazing to see these young children sitting there, at the foothills of the Himalayas, with their eyes closed, listening to the recording in the app with a gentle female voice, fully enraptured. These children looked heavenly and I would have never guessed the hardship, the pain and trauma they had previously endured.

Given the chance, any human can evolve into a greater version of themselves. I was so very grateful that Dwabha had offered me this opportunity. When I heard the children read the introduction of the book, reading my name in Hindi, reading out loud that I was born in the Himalayan Mountains, sent tears flowing down my cheeks. We never know where the inspiration to do something will take us for the greater good of the whole.

My app had brought me here into this classroom with the untouchables. Instead of throwing stones at me because I was white, which happened to me when I was not yet quite three years old in Afghanistan, I now was able to help the less fortunate children to dream, and gave them tools to make their dreams come true. With the help of Dwabha, who truly gave of herself beyond belief, these children now had a chance.

YOU TUBE FILM at RAMANA's SCHOOL

As of this writing, one of her children is now studying to be a pilot in Canada. Another girl became a psychologist.

When we dream big, the universe starts to utilize you as channel – as the hands of God here on Earth – in larger or smaller ways.

THE HOLLYWOOD STAR

On a previous trip to India, we also had stayed at the Divine Resort in Laxman Julah for one month. Time had come again when Don had to fly to Mumbai to teach a workshop on Radionics and I opted to stay in Rishikesh for a few days longer before joining Don on our flight home to Bali.

I had just gotten a massage at the Divine Resort and was sipping my tea to end my massage on a sweet note.

I was seated on a large flow matt and across from me sat an Indian man in his sixties, who was waiting for his friend to finish her massage and he was also sipping on his hot tea slowly. Shortly I struck up a conversation and I realized in moments of poetic silent eye gazing, which he allowed so easily, that we could reach the same realms of heaven in our shared moments of ascension in this silence. It is an art I have described in my book *Dolphins, Love & Destiny*, and let it suffice to say, "It takes one to know one."

We had clicked in our levels of awareness and decided to have lunch together with his partner. While waiting for her, he was a captive audience and I found out amazing things about his life.

His story was breathtaking. As a man in his early thirties he had decided to give up everything – his possessions, his business, and home, to go and live like a recluse in the Himalayan Mountains. And that is what he did for over 25 years, living in the Himalayas on practically nothing, where he never begged, and only took what was offered.

I wanted to ask him about his spiritual journey and about matter, spirit and what his time away from all the commitments of life had taught him. I asked him about his time as a renunciate and how it came about that he was no longer the renunciate. He told me that he had gotten the clear internal message to come back to the world, to teach, to help, to assist others in awakening.

He was like the proverbial yogi that came back down from the mountain, back into the valley to teach, to live his wisdom in the middle of all the temptations and challenges. After 25 years he decided to join regular life again in order to live his mission of helping others reach such states of sublime consciousness.

That was a clear message to me. Stay in the valley with the people! Despite my intermittent feelings of wanting to join the yogis and feeling like I should have a shaven head instead of the long black hair that I did have, I realized early on in my teens that I was here on Earth with a mission.

As we sat sipping our chai, he told me that he was now traveling in the company of a Hollywood photo-model, 30 years his junior but, he assured me, a very spiritual one. After she came out and finished sipping her after-massage-tea, we decided to go off the famous Ramana's Garden, the restaurant run by orphans.

I had gone there for lunch a few days earlier and really wanted to show this place of hope, and home of the untouchables, to this man.

As the three of us, the returned Sadhu-Yogi, the Hollywood photo-model and I, were trying to get a seat in the upstairs deck at Ramana's Garden Restaurant, we noticed the gusts of wind coming up. Quickly the three of us decided to sit downstairs, inside, rather than on the open balcony. On comfortable cushions, cross-legged, at low level tables, we were protected from the wind and the rain.

Shortly this little room was full to the brim with guests, wildly dressed, many visiting the International Yoga Festival that happens in Rishikesh every year around the beginning of March. Everyone was trying to find a small spot at a table to eat, trying to stay dry and warm inside.

As we were all huddling inside the little room, I tried to position our threesome in such a way that I could sit next to the yogi. But alas, due to too many people streaming in, we all needed to shuffle around to accommodate everyone. I wound up sitting on the far end way from my new-found yogi friend.

Suddenly, another group entered and a woman with angelic large brown eyes took a seat near us. Quickly we started up a conversation between all of us at that end of the table and I found out that she was helping movie script writers in Hollywood to write about socially impactful stories in order to make a change on this planet with their powerful skills as a script writer. What a story. What a mission, I marveled!

I was mesmerized by her loving eyes and by her story. Quickly I reasoned that if there was a script to be written, it should be about Ramana's Garden. I had heard some hair-raising stories by the mother Theresa of this place, Deva Dwabha, and her story needed to be heard.

But, alas, the blonde photo-model who was the partner of the yogi, was asking a million questions of this brown eyed angel and quickly monopolized the conversation with her own talk of her connections in Hollywood.

Off they were, talking about the dinners they had attended with this or that famous actor and I could not keep up with that kind of talk. Quickly I realized that my Hollywood contacts didn't measure up.

Here was a real show of who is who and who knows whom. I was a bit heartbroken that I could not talk more with this angelic woman who looked like she truly lived a life of service and luminosity.

I have to admit, not being able to drop all those names and being overshadowed by the photo-model who had positioned herself between me and the yogi so that I could not talk to him nor to the angel, I got a taste for what it feels like when people vie for power and over-shadow others. I personally like to have a conversation go round in a circle. Everyone has something valuable to contribute, but this was not the case today. It was a show of who-is-in-the-know. And I was definitely not. I sur-rendered to the sabotaged conversations I had hoped to have had.

The day ended with a heavy feeling in my stomach and I never got a chance to exchange phone numbers or email addresses with the angelic woman who helped so many people. I am not sure exactly why I wanted to be in touch with her or for what reason, but it was a sense of deep appreciation and adoration of her light that stayed with me the entire year to come. There are sometimes when something needs to be shared, needs to be said, or needs to be heard. And that had not happened today.

For whatever reason, for the following year, she had stayed in my heart and soul.

MEETING THE FILM ANGEL from HOLLYWOOD AGAIN

A year later, I wanted to show Don the wonderful Ramana's Garden. We stood in line to order our meals in this make-shift, cozy restaurant, school and haven for the orphans. Just as we were about to take our seat to have a little visit with Dwabha, who had become friends with me over the last year, my eyes fell on a woman with large brown eyes. It was the same woman whom I had met a year before here. Indeed it was that radiant angel, Sandra from California, the woman who had helped script writers to make socially impactful movies.

As I found out later, she had come to attend the annual International Yoga Festival in Rishikesh a few days early because she was in the process of filming yogis and saints for the upcoming Online Yoga Summit offered by The Shift Network.

Instantly I jumped up to greet her and told her what a deep impression her presence had made on me and told her how she had never left my mind and heart and how her light had touched me.

I told her about the amazing story behind Dwabha's life and the orphanage which I will share with you in the next chapter, and I told her how I felt that this story would be a great inspiration to her script writers.

Was this the purpose of my meeting with her, the one thing that had not been said?

Sometimes when I am in a conversation that doesn't seem to want to end, and yet I feel like leaving, I often ask myself: "What has not been said? What have I not heard or shared?" This question or answer was obviously persistent and presented me with the same opportunity just one year later.

One thing led to the next and then we exchanged our contact information. A feeling of seeing each other again was in the air.

This angel Sandra, indeed set up a time to interview Dwabha on film, and a meeting for the following summer in California was arranged as well. This was making my heart sing. For some reason I felt I wanted to assist in getting the message out to the world about Ramana's Garden. This was a great avenue.

And a bonus came out for me as well! Sandra needed more people for her interviews of the yogis and teachers for the upcoming online Yoga Summit. She asked me if she could interview me for a short segment for the online Yoga Summit, on the theme of Seva, or service. Service is something you give when you are filled with whatever you really need. It is the overflowing cup that has extra to share.

Seva is an aspect of spiritual evolution thought to purify the mind and heart. Seva, service, is what you do when you want to create a positive spin in your life. Service is a sign that you are beyond the (what my mom would call potentially narcissistic) state of staring at your own navel.

The day we met again, I had just given my children's book *Alin Learns to Use His Imagination*, a book about a fairytale with embedded psychotherapeutic techniques, to a classroom full of eager Indian children at Ramana's school.

Sandra, the Hollywood angel, had decided that she wanted me to give a short interview about doing yoga, the spiritual path and doing service. The interview was aired later in that year at the Online Yoga Summit by The Shift Network.

Whatever it was that had attracted me to Sandra and the yearning to connect to her had stayed with me for the entire year. Our deepest thoughts and what we hold in our hearts and minds will set up the realities around us. Seeming miracles or for that matter what looks like chance meetings, are all orchestrated by our innermost dreams and what we hold in our hearts.

A PALACE FOR A PRINCESS

I was about to teach a *Living From Vision®* Teacher Training seminar at our *Shambala Retreat Center* in Bali. On the north shore of Bali, the ocean lapping at our feet, and dolphins swimming by at a distance, *Shambala* really had become a Heaven on Earth.

Han Ye and her husband Wang Gang and another friend of theirs had come all the way from mainland China to Bali in order to become **Living From Vision®** teachers. We had published the LFV workbooks in Chinese just in time for the teacher training, including 12 guided imagery exercises in Chinese which were part of the companion LFV app. I was very excited to see *Living From Vision®* being practiced in China.

We only had three Chinese students and the rest were either German or English speaking. To make sure they felt welcomed and supported, I joined them now and then for lunch. I had noticed that Han Ye had been somewhat listless since she arrived. *Why would that be*, I wondered? She had come all the way from China to Bali in order to become an LFV teacher. Yet she was somewhat unengaged in creating a beautiful future for herself.

Over lunch she told me her reason: She had participated in a seminar in China recently, where they were told to question their identity to the core. The intent was actually rather good. The teacher wanted the students to reach into the core of themselves so they could discover that they are not the personality, but rather they were the soul. He tried to do it by bashing everything that a person might ordinarily identify with as being the self. They went through exercises where they could realize that they were neither their clothing, nor their personality, nor their job description, nor their family, neither rich nor poor. In the end Han Ye was left with a feeling of being NOTHING, and nothing she had ever valued up to this point had been important. A huge emptiness engulfed her.

Instead of reaching into the level beyond that into the soul levels, she kept dwelling in this nothingness. Instead of fullness, she experienced an emptiness. She had landed in the proverbial black tunnel sometimes called the Bardo or the world in between the worlds. Some meditation teachers aim at staying in this undefined nothingness. I agree it has its purpose. We need to realize that we are MORE than our body. But our beautiful Han Ye had somehow integrated this nothingness so deeply that she had lost the taste for life.

Regarding this world as illusion or as Maya, as Indians call it, can be misleading. Illusion has a very bad connotation. It can make one feel like it's useless or counterproductive to focus on the world that surrounds us since after all it's just the world of appearances, right?

However it is the love, the connection, the work we do for others, the discovery that we can create, and the discovery that we are connected to the source which makes this life worth living. If we were on Earth and disregarded everything as being simply useless and illusionary and we would therefore give up engaging in life, we would not grow. Our soul needs the grit that duality can provide. This is where we find the true power of our light, the true power of our love. Without any challenges, like gravity, we would not build any muscle, emotional, mental or spiritual.

Seeing her listlessness I engaged Han Ye in a couple of discussions and bit by bit her juices started flowing again.

And then there was a turnaround moment. I sat with Han Ye and her husband at the restaurant at *Shambala Retreat Center*. The blue ocean was just an arm's length away, lapping the shore. Palm trees were swaying in the wind and we literally sat in a little bubble of Heaven on Earth.

During the previous session she had completed during the LFV teacher training, she had been asked to dream big.

So I asked her what her biggest dream was. At first she gave me some reasonably good big dreams. You know, the kind of decent dreams that a person should have, like a good job, a family and a house.

But then I probed more deeply and asked her what she really wanted if money was absolutely not an issue or any other lack of resources.

Suddenly she was fully excited and she described her grand vision in full color: She wanted to have a Retreat Center in a very pristine part of China. She saw a Retreat Center with mountains and trees surrounding her. China, as you might know, has been very polluted, especially in the big cities, and she had grown tired of living in this pollution.

Her dream was to have her own Retreat Center and to live in Heaven on Earth.

I encouraged her in her dream, which she put out into the imaginary distant future. But for the moment, she really felt it in vivid colors around her. It was remarkable how lit she was compared to the few days beforehand when she had been feeling listless.

I know exactly what amount of resources and effort and energy it takes to create a retreat center, as Don and I had built our *Shambala Retreat Center* from the ground up. But I totally supported her because she was finally fully alive.

It is important for all of us to remember that we do have deep dreams that really matter to our hearts. Dreams that excite our souls and that make us feel like it's worth living for.

After the seminar Han Ye and her husband Wang Gang and her friend went back to China and taught a small class of Chinese students. Months later they sent me a PDF with the most stunning feedback they had gotten from their Chinese students. This was a new approach to life for many of them. To learn to dream big and learn to feel one's own ambitions had been suppressed for decades in China.

But as we know, neither suppression of dreams nor indulgence actually is the truth. It is the light that illuminates our show here on earth which we get to know and learn to cherish. Until we learn to touch into the source of life, the life force often times remains invisible until we ask. That is when the magic happens.

Their main focus of work however was at their research institute which was employing radionic equipment to grow amazing organic vegetables in otherwise barren soil as well as work with alternative healing methods. Their institute had created miracles that people thought were impossible. Over a period of two years they did research on over 30,000 people with laboratory tests to prove that when they were administered radionically charged water, the people healed.

They also grew more vegetables than anybody could ever envision in barren soil without the use of fertilizers, and outperformed their neighboring farmers who used all the chemical help they could get. Their food sold out faster because it tasted better, was stronger, didn't decay as fast as other farmers' foods, and qualified for the organic label.

Five months later, the four of us are walking up the street in Rishikesh to see my favorite sadhu. I wanted to show them the famous orphanage and restaurant called Ramana's Garden, which I described to you already.

The two of them had come to Rishikesh to meet up with us because they were going to travel to Mumbai and give a presentation at Don's SE-5 seminar on the results of the radionic equipment they used in their agriculture. They were equipped with slides, images and proof to show how barren soil had been turned into the most luscious environment of magical gardens and agriculture. Truly a Findhorn miracle.

Don and I have been working with the SE-5 since 1986.

In the midst of the holy cows, the wafting of the incense smells and the honking of the motorbikes passing by, we were engulfed in the most magical conversation.

Time stopped as I listened to their story unfold.

Some months after they had gone back to China, officials from the Chinese government had approached her and her husband because they wanted to gift them the most precious mountaintop with an already built retreat center as a gift.

This mountaintop was no ordinary mountaintop. The rugged outcropping was reserved for the most prestigious to visit, previously reserved only for princesses. In the past, no ordinary folk were allowed onto the mountain, and nobody to this day has been allowed to purchase this land.

The entire mountain has been considered holy, only fit for princesses. When Han Ye and Wang Gang were approached to move their institute into this very location they were speechless.

However it wasn't until I exclaimed in astonishment, "You got your retreat center in just a few months!", that they realized that they had actually envisioned having a retreat center and this was the universe's way of responding to their very wish.

There was a deep lesson in this for me. Han Ye does look like a princess to me when I look at her. Maybe it's just my eyes, but it's the air with which she walks. Not that she has her head up too high, but more like the deep expectation of spirit to use only the best that is deeply embedded in her subconscious.

Her father always lavished her with positive energy, supporting her in whatever she wished. He'd come from incredibly poor circumstances and had been blessed enough to be given a coal mine when he was a very young man, based on the merits of his good character.

The good karma that he encountered was a reflection of his inner core goodness. It was this inner core of goodness he had passed on to his daughter.

Her self-image, her positive beliefs and her expectation that only the greatest things will happen to her in her life created an aura of unbeatable success around her. She was willing to work hard, create a vision and go for it. But she hadn't even realized how quickly the universe had answered her deepest dream. And remember this deepest dream evolved during the seminar where she was still digesting that this life was merely an illusion.

She had gotten over this feeling that this life on Earth was illusionary. Yes, focusing on our soul as the core center of ourselves, gives us the power to create miracles. And yes, we don't need to focus on the outside in order to create something magical. We need to go within and create the miracle first inside.

Life on Earth is a phenomenal school. I like to call it the "Schoolhouse Earth". We grow through every single step with take. We evolve in the brilliance of our soul's awareness. The brighter we get, the more connected we get to the source, the faster the miracle.

We expand our light body, our time-space body with every experience. The brilliance of our soul-diamond starts shining in every nook and cranny of our subconscious, conscious and superconscious. Here on Earth, our subconsciously held beliefs create the shape that the light takes on and manifests.

So dare to dream, follow what is truly exciting to your heart. These dreams will take on shape and form of the expression of your mission and purpose in life.

THE BIG SECRET

Have you ever manifested a parking spot when you needed one? Many people have had some success with manifesting at least some things. Yet there remain questions about how to manifest effectively, why it can happen and how it works. Today I want to take you on a journey into discovering an even bigger secret.

To find out just how big the secret is, join me on a journey to Hawaii in a moment! This chapter was included in the bestselling book – **THE BIG SECRET** –with Jack Canfield. The title of the chapter is called DREAM BIG – THE UNIVERSE IS LISTENING, just like this book.

But first let me summarize how far we have come in our understanding of the universe so far.

The book and movie *The Secret* has rekindled the desire to understand the hidden and ancient laws of the universe. These ancient laws reveal that we are not just physical bodies, nor mere cogs in the wheel of life.

However, during the last 800 years, and especially in the era of Enlightenment, human kind has been obsessed with discovering repeatable laws of nature and rather pursued the scientific understanding of the universe, which brought us the body-mind split.

In our modern age this has brought us space travel and the internet. We have externalized our thinking abilities and created a huge empire of "things". Many thought leaders now seriously consider that the mind is the equivalent of consciousness and that it maybe transferable into a computer. The Transhumanist movement is trying to suggest the use of sophisticated technologies to greatly enhance human intellectual, physical, and psychological capacities, opening the doors to the creation of cyborgs. Even Elon Musk, the inventor of the Tesla car and co-founder of PayPal and Space X, believes it is our only chance to survive the advent of AI (Artificial Intelligence). They promote the creation of an Übermensch, a world where God is dead and the Soul is but an aspect of the body. **AI,** cyborgs and robots are the epitome of this kind of thinking.

And yet, you and I are here because we have discovered that there is a very different kind of universe afoot. We can affect change in the matrix of time-space through our focused attention, *The Secret* says.

Many of us are slowly discovering the deeper nature of the universe and quantum physicists are puzzled.

It is likely that you are part of this movement of pioneers that is on the brink of discovering the bigger secrets of the universe.

Let us start with religions. All religions have in common that they teach us that we can talk to God, the universe, or various deities. They teach that our thoughts can have effect. The fact that our prayers are answered and that we can witness magical results down here on Earth due to our conscious focus, is in itself a mind boggling feat. Think about it! It implies that we are truly living in a dreaming matrix rather than a solid state universe. We are indeed living in a consciousness-interactive universe, as plenty of miracle stories from all over the world prove to us.

Just how do you and I take part in this discovery of this greater universe? And what is **THE BIG SECRET?** Join me now on the journey to Hawaii.

My husband and I lived on the Big Island of Hawaii for a good part of 12 years doing research with wild dolphins, about their telepathic and other extraordinary healing effects. I chronicled these amazing encounters and lessons I learned from the dolphins in two of my books, called *Wisdom of the Dolphins*and *Dolphins, Love and Destiny*.

On this day, Don and I were driving back "Home" from the airport, ready to be back into the swing of our island life on Hawaii. We had been gone for over four months, being on a seminar tour through Europe. Close to our house, just a few streets away, was a dolphin beach where dolphins frequently came into a little-known bay.

Just as we turned onto our road which was bordering onto a National Forest Reserve, we had to face a shocking view: Three abandoned cars that had been dropped off onto our street in our absence, had turned our paradise into a junk yard.

As we got out of our car, our nearly toothless neighbor greeted us. In her scratchy voice she bemoaned, "I have called the cops, the city, everyone, over and over for the last three months to come pick up these Junkers but no results. They just don't care."

The state of Hawaii was, in fact, known for not bothering to clean all the streets, especially in the more rural areas, and many old relics of junk cars had already remained on the roadside for decades.

Today I was not taking NO for an answer. There had to be a way to have my paradise back. My emotions were upset and I was not happy.

However, I firmly belied by now that all possibilities exist simultaneously, as Hugh Everett and Wheeler postulated in their interpretation of Quantum Physics, saying **that "many parallel realities exist simultaneously."**

Also Brian Greene has postulated in the Super String Theory that there are extra dimensions of space-time. The new scientific thinking is indeed pointing to a reality that is far beyond the atomic model that has dominated our minds until now. **Science is starting to meet magic.**

Quantum physics has proven in experiments (EPR Experiment, etc.]) that our consciousness or our focused attention is part and parcel of crafting the outcome, at least at the microcosmic level.

I had already experienced that a change in myself could create a change in the macrocosm that surrounds me, if I simply tune into the universe of my choice and dip the cup of my awareness into the ocean of the many parallel choices.

Looking at the junk cars, I instantly wondered if there was anything that I had done wrong. Before approaching the universe with a request for a bigger miracle, we need to have a **positive balance on our** *Karmic Credit Card*. This may or may not be news to you, but a clear conscience is a prerequisite for an extraordinary and magical life.

Don and I took our luggage into our house and as

quickly as I could, I arranged my little meditation room and lit a candle.

After having calmed my mind and body, I started by dropping my brainwave state down into the Alpha and Theta levels, which are around 4–8 HZ. This is the mind-set that is usually associated with meditation. However, this is only the launching pad for reaching even greater awareness states.

As I entered a clearer, calmer state of mind, I started pulling up into higher gamma brainwaves (22 HZ to 100 HZ, but usually centering our 40+ HZ).

"Research in gamma-band oscillations may explain the heightened sense of consciousness, bliss and intellectual acuity subsequent to meditation," says the Wikipedia.

That day, I simply imagined that I was raising my innermost core of awareness, my soul, to the highest point in the universe. This has the side effect of raising our brainwave frequency into the Gamma range. I aimed at entering the point of singularity. This is where I feel God and I are one. Some people say they imagine being a rocket or a beam of light that flies and unites with the center of creation.

Once I was in that pristine state of heightened stillness, I nearly forgot my deepest wish of that day. But I pulled all my awareness together and remembered that I was on a mission and wanted to land my rocket ship in a parallel universe, one in which the street was returned to my **Heaven on Earth.**

Despite the outer negative circumstances, I **re-focused** on **the end-result** that I really wanted **while**

in this singularity state. I could liken this shifting to rearranging the matrix around me until it fitted my sense of alignment.

Requests for larger miracles that deeply matter to us have the fuel needed to shift the blueprint of life. The request will have the required energy to enter into the eye of the needle and to come out on the other side of the looking glass, allowing you to appear in the parallel world of your choice.

In this heightened state of awareness, while being deeply relaxed and focused into oneness, I witnessed the return of my paradise in my inner vision. I imagined that I was entering the hologram of my pristine Heaven on Earth, complete with a clean street.

I had once read somewhere that at moments of 100% certainty, a supernatural feeling sets in. This lets people know that they are completely on target. I entered into this reverie until I had that 100% feeling of certainty.

When my inner image of my desired future really hit the perfect resonant spot in the cosmos, it indicated to me that my vision of my perfect future was about to manifest. This inner certainty is far different from going out on a limb of faith, and buying things on a credit card with the firm assumption that the money will follow, which people commonly do.

A precise alignment is needed for the perfect outcome to manifest in the external world. We have to know for sure, when wehave arrived at the right portal of the parallel dimension of our choice. Indeed, we need to know when we have reached the time-space that holds the fulfillment of our dream.

When we set the dial of time-space onto the desired coordinates, we do this in our body, mind and soul. Our entire self is vibrating to a higher tune at that moment.

Actually, we already do this with every single thought and feeling every minute of the day, albeit often unconsciously, or with expectations that are shaped by our culture.

However, the more you and I are awakened to this co-creative process of becoming a conscious dreamer, the better the outcomes. When we awaken to the fact that we are dreaming, we are increasingly free to live the life of our dreams.

We have to set our focus on a desired outcome and notice when the resonant peak with the cosmos has been reached. As we are more experienced, life will flow more and more gracefully and our mere thoughts will unfold as perfect creations before us, removing even the need to create any changes.

While still sitting in my meditation room in Hawaii I suddenly heard some crunchy metallic sounds. *Could that be trucks coming to pick up those cars already?* I marveled. I thought to myself, *Better not check, simply keep meditating.* As the saying goes: *"A watched pot never boils."* We need to let go and let God.

After all, at the end of our short street, a house was being built using a crane. It might just be the workers creating the crunchy sounds, I reasoned.

After finishing my meditation, Don and I drove to our little hippie town calledPahoa to have dinner, as our refrigerator and stomachs both were empty.

I totally forgot to check up on my experiment as we drove out onto our street. But on our way back home that night, I made sure to check on my reality. Had it shifted as the sounds had almost indicated to me, or not?

SUCCESS! Our street was again back to its perfect state of pristine perfection, and my paradise was back in order.

Initially, I questioned the miracle and did what most readers might be doing right now: I wondered if this miracle was a mere coincidence and I briefly looked for a logical answer.

But then I quickly recalled the many other miracles which I had already experienced. I remembered my lesson from long ago: Logic wants to have a neat and orderly progression of cause and effect. **However, miracles don't happen in a logical sequence. Miracles depend on our ability to lift ourselves outside of the ordinary logical time-space sequence.**

Logic is the basis of our scientific world view and has its place.

However, the BIG SECRET is that we don't live in a solid world nor a solid reality. We manifest those circumstances that are in keeping with our beliefs and our vibrational state. Once you learn that you are the creator of your life, you will have liberties and abilities that far surpass the normal laws of physics.

In the beginning, learning to manifest is about mastering your ability to focus and raising your vibration. It is about learning that your conscious and subconscious mind affect your reality.

When you master that, you will realize that **life is a living hologram**. You then become the conscious time-space co-creator and director of your life. The frequency of your soul will be reflected in what you manifest around you. We live in a Multiverse, and you live in your version of Heaven on Earth.

Happiness and feelings of bliss will let you know when you are on the right path. Pain, unhappiness and even suffering will let you know when you are out of phase with life.

We all want to manifest a better life with more money, greater health, and a soulmate. And YES this is all possible.

However, please remember: Life is not about manifesting "things". Our increased manifestation skills are a side effect of raising our vibration. That is what evolution is about.

Shining greater light and more love is the real purpose of our life. As you evolve, the world around you will reflect more love and light back to you.

STOP – LOOK – and CHOOSE. Any moment of life you can step out of the film that you are currently living in and become aware that you are the director. You can **refocus on what you really want.** You sit in the director's chair of your life. Increased bliss and happiness will be your rewards.

Remember: Dare to dream big, THE UNIVERSE IS LISTENING.

Why did I tell you the car story? Read on.....

STEPS TO CREATING MIRACLES

I wanted to tell you the car story in order to demonstrate the use of the imagination with a regular day-to-day event. We all encounter moments that are less than desirable. At the moment we had just arrived in Hawaii, cleansing the street of those three Junker cars was a goal that seemed impossible. Yet I didn't give up. Of course I had practiced many times, in many situations and this was not my first attempt.

Given that our neighbor had already called on the authorities to help clean the street to no avail for three months and the fact that lots of other places around this area of Hawaii still had plenty of abandoned cars alongside the roads, trying to manifest a clean street was a bit of a stretch. However, we are all here to realize that we live in a co-creative universe and that we need to *claim our birthright to live in paradise.*

How many times do you run into a situation that is less than satisfying? By not giving into a sob story, not playing the victim or feeling defeated you can realize that everything around you is an expression of consciousness. Whatever you can change in your inner world first, you can change in your outer world. By making lemonade when handed lemons, you grow into a bigger, greater being. You co-create Heaven on Earth.

While sitting down in Hawaii and re-imagining my surroundings, a truck had come to pick up the cars. The

240

fact that this change of my world happened within 30 minutes qualified in my book as miraculous. If I can do it, you can do it – as many others since then have done also!

In order to manifest miracles in our daily life, all it takes is wanting to create something that you *truly* desire. If you feel in your heart that your wish is true and worthy, *you will get results.*

By reading success stories of other people, we subconsciously start opening our inner doors to the possibility. We are opening to the higher forces. We start believing that such things might be possible for us as well. We start trusting that good things and miraculous things can and do happen. Our mind and attention can help shape the reality around us on this planet.

Wishing for something that is truly in alignment with your heart, mind and soul:

There are of course rules as to how to effectively manifest miracles:

First, we **truly** have to desire something.

Second, it has to be very meaningful for us.

Third, it has to be believable to us in some way. (With practice our capacities expand and our miraculous outreach grows larger).

Fourth, we need feel that our wish is in harmony with our soul.

If living in a castle makes us feel that we will be able to further our soul's purpose here on Earth, we will manifest that castle. However if somewhere inside of ourself we have the subtle feeling that it might detract us, and our soul evolution is paramount to us, creating a castle will be in opposition to our soul's aspiration. It is not the castle or the creation thereof that is the question. The only question is whether our wishes are in alignment with our deepest core and values.

Believable

There is the old adage, 'seeing is believing'. Make use of that. Create small miracles that are based on something that you find easy to believe, because perhaps a friend of yours has done it or maybe because something inside of you tells you that you can do it. Build upon experience.

Explore and experiment with feeling the feedback from the universe, learning to understand the dialogue between you and the larger field, discovering how you actually enter into it multidimensional universe with your energy and awareness. When you may contact it is a distinct feeling. And this ability will expand over time, and the depth that you can reach within this universe will expand.

Our imagination will bring about the results we look for in a way that is harmonious with our beliefs. Healing can happen many ways. Remember that it is our job to invent the future. It will happen in accordance with our beliefs.

The more you practice and the realize that we do live in a dreaming universe, the more you will allow your-self to achieve whatever it is you want. The old laws by which you thought the universe was operating, slowly change to allow for more and more miraculous manifestation. But to you they will simply feel natural, because they only happen when you feel that they should.

On one hand it is rather easy. In essence, you need to remember to imagine yourself in a beautiful movie, with feelings of fulfillment. Every time you see yourself watching a tragic drama of yourself, stop the thought, re-envision what you really want and give that image and feeling your emotional 'yes'.

Sooner or later we will realize that we do not have the luxury to afford a negative thought and instead we learn to create positive outward pouring energy.

The second step is learning how to deal with the negative feelings and beliefs that pull you in the opposite direction of your desires.

The third step, and in actuality the very first step to be done, is to align yourself with your highest source, your soul, the diamond of light within you, to make sure that your wishes are in alignment with the fundamental YOU.

One of the main ingredients in the recipe to manifestation is the strength of your belief. We learn to believe and we learn to trust in a higher force. We can open to receiving that extra magical power by believing something to be true. But that is something that we cannot talk ourselves into. This belief comes from experience and from hearing of other's successes, others, who are human like us and who have created a miracles in their lives before.

This book is about learning that we live in a dreamtime matrix. Even more so, this book is about the fact that we essentially are pure consciousness and that our awareness can create changes and effects in the manifest world around us.

The carrot of manifesting our dreams eventually leads us to a greater and deeper understanding of the nature of the universe and essentially guides us towards ascension of our consciousness. As we bridge the awareness of being a self with a body and rise to the awareness of being an energy being, it essentially leads us onwards to the realization that we are pure information and beyond that, absolute brilliant pure consciousness unified with the entire field of All That Is.

By using their dreaming mind, the Aborigine's desire to find a waterhole lead them to being able to speak to the clouds and make rain when needed. They used the dreamtime to be at the right place and the right time and mold the dream fabric, which we call reality, to be in the highest alignment with their visions, talents and their purpose in life.

In our awareness we are connected to the larger picture. We are connected the evolution of mankind, to the mass dream of our collective as well as our personal enlightenment. In that sense, each and every one of us furthers the evolution of all of mankind by becoming a radiant beacon of consciousness that springs forth like a well. You become a fountain of light to others and inspire everyone whom you touch.

Learning how to manifest within the dream matrix called time-space is part and parcel of living as an enlightened being. Manifesting is not an end in and of itself, it is one of the steps of awakening to the higher order of being here on Earth.

Magical things will happen along the way as we move through the different stages and it is good to understand right from the start that evolution of ourselves means to evolve each aspect of ourselves.

It is equally important to master the ability to navigate time-space on the earthly plane and to know how to manifest as well as be able to enter into the highest states of consciousness and reach into enlightenment. We need to be walking with our feet on the Earth and our heads in the Heavens.

But how do we live in Heaven on Earth when we are oftentimes surrounded by undesirable things and events?

WHEN THINGS AREN'T WORKING

The Conscious, Subconscious, and the Superconscious:

In most ancient traditions, consciousness has been divided into three realms. One – the consciousness of the lower realms, namely the subconscious; Two – the realm of the day to day life which is the ordinary daytime consciousness, and; Three – the realms of the divine, the super-conscious.

The evolution of our consciousness requires that we handle all the levels of consciousness such as the deeper recesses of our mind. This includes our emotional mind, beliefs, traumas, and undigested experiences, as well as reaching upward into the higher capacities of our consciousness into the superconscious and into the ever higher dimensions. We ignite ourselves as we move through our evolution to the increasingly finer dimensions within us, until we enter through the Eye-of-God into the Unified Field.

245

Our subconscious mind is busy creating even though our conscious mind might be thinking of something completely different. Consciously we might be wishing for a good job but subconsciously we might be feeling doubtful, afraid or worried. If we attempt to focus on the goal that is larger than we are used to, often times we are confronted with our unconsciously held beliefs that are in the way.

Each time we are faced with something that is not quite the way we would like it to be, we also have the opportunity to ascend in our frequency, rise to a higher purpose of our humanness and co-create Heaven on Earth. It takes extra energy and a complete commitment to being the creator within one's own life. Playing the victim might be easier, but is by far more painful. The benefits of choosing to be the co-creator of our life are obvious. If we are the creator, we can make a change. No matter what the situation around us looks like, eventually we can re-create the dream until it becomes beautiful and completely in alignment with our highest soul's aspiration.

Here are four steps for super charging a goal:

- Discover a meaningful goal or wish that you wish to do, be, or have.

- Describe your goal or wish in a sentence.

- Imagine how it would be if it were already fulfilled. Run a little movie in your mind.

- Feel it, as it would feel if this wish was already fulfilled, until your body says YES that is IT!

- Connect to a higher source.

  (Make it a habit to read books that inspire you and speak about the power of the universe).

- Surrender your wish to this higher energy and let go. Let God.

- Finally, know that it will happen in its right time.

Most importantly: Let God do the miracle of arranging the entire universe to make your creative vision come true.

Remember, that you will succeed even more if you are in alignment with your deeper values that contribute to the evolution of yourself, the goodness of life, and others around you.

ISLANDS OF LIGHT
Excerpt from the film
MY DINNER WITH ANDRE

In a film titled *My Dinner With Andre,*which was released in 1981 I found great wisdom that summarized two bold points we might want to all consider.

In the film, two old friends by the name of Wallace (Wallace Shawn) and Andre (Andre Gregory), who haven't seen each other for five years, agree to meet for dinner.

Andre, a once well-known theater director, dropped out of the New York scene to travel the world, whereas Wallace stuck around and only found mixed success as a playwright.

As they sit down to eat, Andre launches into a series of fantastic stories from his time away and Wallace can't help but notice how different their world views have become.

On this website, This Is What Highly Conscious People Talk About I found a great comment about the very excerpt that I want to share with you.

In their words:

"The following is an excerpt from the movie My Dinner with André *where once again, an important message is*

hidden in plain sight. Pay close attention to the part where Andre talks about the pockets of light appearing all around the world because this is happening right now as each person awakens.

And as each person awakens, it changes the outcome of probable timelines in parallel universes and alternate realities.*Right now, we are playing out the greatest probability of all possible scenarios in this particular reality, but as more people awaken and change their views on how they see reality, the reality changes with it."*

Reading this dialog of **My Dinner with Andre**, 36 years after its release, I see that much of what Andre shares has become even truer today than it might've already been back in 1981.

The message is clear: Wake up while you can. You can become that pocket of light that shifts reality into a positive direction. As you will read in the following chapter THE GLOBAL BRAIN, we are indeed much more powerful than we might imagine.

First let me share an excerpt from their dialogue:

Wally: Well, why...why do you think that is? [We are not sure what exactly he is referring to, but it will become clearer in a moment]

Wally: I mean, why is that, I mean, is it just because people are...are lazy today, or they're bored? I mean, are we just like bored, spoiled children who've just been lying in the bathtub all day just playing with their plastic duck, and now they're just thinking,

"Well, what can I do?"

Andre: Okay. Yes. We're bored. We're all bored now. But has it ever occurred to you, Wally that the process that creates this boredom that we see in the world now may very well be a self-perpetuating, unconscious form of brainwashing created by a world totalitarian government based on money? And that all of this is much more dangerous than one thinks? And it's not just a question of individual survival Wally, but that somebody who's bored is asleep? And somebody who's asleep will not say "no"?

Andre: See, I keep meeting these people, I mean, uh, just a few days ago I met this man whom I greatly admire, he's a Swedish physicist, Gustav Björnstrand, and he told me that he no longer watches television, he doesn't read newspapers and he doesn't read magazines. He's completely cut them out of his life because he really does feel that we're living in some kind of Orwellian nightmare now, and that everything that you hear now contributes to turning you into a robot.

And when I was at Findhorn, I met this extraordinary English tree expert who had devoted his life to saving trees. Just got back from Washington, lobbying to save the Redwoods, he's 84 years old, and he always travels with a backpack because he never knows where he's gonna be tomorrow. And when I met him at Findhorn, he said to me, "Where are you from?" and I said, "New York." He said, "Ah, New York. Yes, that's a very interesting place. Do you know a lot of New Yorkers who keep talking about the fact that they want to leave, but never do?" And I said, "Oh, yes." And he said, "Why do you think they don't leave?" I gave him different banal theories. He said, "Oh, I don't think it's that way at all."

He said, "I think that New York is the new model for the new concentration camp, where the camp has been built by the inmates themselves, and the inmates are the guards, and they have this pride in this thing they've built. They've built their own prison. And so they exist in a state of schizophrenia where they are both guards and prisoners, and as a result, they no longer have, having been lobotomized, the capacity to leave the prison they've made or to even see it as a prison." And then he went into his pocket, and he took out a seed for a tree and he said, "This is a pine tree." He put it in my hand and he said, "Escape before it's too late."

See, actually, for two or three years now, Chiquita and I have had this very unpleasant feeling that we really should get out. That we really should feel like Jews in Germany in the late 1930s. Get out of here. Of course, the problem is where to go, because it seems quite obvious that the whole world is going in the same direction. See, I think it's quite possible that the 1960s represented the last burst of the human being before he was extinguished and that this is the beginning of the rest of the future now, and that, from now on there'll simply be all these robots walking around, feeling nothing, thinking nothing. And there'll be nobody left to remind them that there once was a species called a human being, with feelings and thoughts, and that history and memory are right now being erased, and soon nobody will really remember that life existed on the planet.

Now, of course, Björnstrand feels that there's really almost no hope. And that we're probably going back to a very savage, lawless, terrifying period.

Findhorn people see it a little differently. They're feeling that there'll be these "pockets of light" springing up in different parts of the world, and that these will be, in a way, invisible planets on this planet, and that as we, or the world, grow colder, we can take invisible space journeys to these different planets, refuel for what it is we need to do on the planet itself, and come back.And it's their feeling that there have to be centers, now, where people can come and reconstruct a new future for the world. And when I was talking to Gustav Björnstrand, he was saying that actually, these centers are growing up everywhere now!

And that's what they're trying to do, which is what Findhorn was trying to do, and in a way what I was trying to do...I mean, these things can't be given names, but in a way, these are all attempts at creating a new kind of school, or a new kind of monastery.

And Björnstrand talks about the concept of reserves, islands of safety, where history can be remembered, and the human being can continue to function in order to maintain the species through a dark age.In other words, we're talking about an underground, which did exist in a different way during the Dark Ages among the mystical orders of the Church.

And the purpose of this underground is to find out how to preserve the light, life, the culture. How to keep things living.

You see, I keep thinking that what we need is a new language, a language of the heart, languages in the Polish forest where language wasn't needed. Some kind of language between people that is a new kind of poetry, that's the poetry of the dancing bee that tells us where the honey is.

And I think that in order to create that language, you're going to have to learn how you can go through a looking glass into another kind of perception, where you have that sense of being united to all things. And suddenly, you understand everything. And thus ends the dialog.

That short segment out of the TV show 'My Dinner With Andre' spoke of some fundamental human issues, that are as old as time. The unaware and unawake human, the islands of light, it all exists because we are here on Earth in a sort of Earth school. The purpose of life is to awaken to a greater level of reality and to become filled with love and light. Reincarnation makes it so that we are all at different stages of illumination, wakefulness and capacity to shine light.

FIRST STEPS TO AWAKENING

Just like Andre shared, the TV has hypnotizedmost people. Getting rid of the TV and furthermore, unplugging from the news, unplugging from the mass media, is the first step to create the kind of mental and emotional space you need to co-create a better world.

Who can become aware of their own co-creative power under a continuous onslaught of negativity, which is keeping the mind in a well-orchestrated polarization? The well-coordinated events of negativity pull many into predictable reactions. The old adage*"divide and conquer"* still holds true today. Be careful what side you fall for when watching the news. Most of the news is intentionally orchestrated and intelligently coordinated in order to create discord, often with a desired reaction in mind.

I hope you can see through the charade. Everybody needs to be alert so they don't fall for the psychological fodder, but instead be a beacon of light. If you meditate sufficiently you will know the news from within. You will also find the right news falling into your lap at the right time.

It might be better to move out of the rat race and leave the hypnotic lifestyle behind, leave the world that is lifeless and trade it in for an awake presence in which you can create from within.

THE UNIVERSE IS LISTENING and you can be a co-creative lighthouse on this planet. Once you master the process of living radiantly and co-creatively in a beautiful world, living in your own Heaven on Earth, you can then start becoming an agent of positive change for a greater field around you.

FINDHORN and the ISLANDS of LIGHT

Remember how I started my book out? The quests for the hidden mystery teachings and the Heaven on Earth which was thought to be in Shambala.

254

We run a spiritual teaching center in Bali called *Shambala Oceanside Retreat* which indeed is such an island of light, one of many islands like this across the planet.

Remember my fascination with Findhorn, a place where vegetables were grown without the use of fertilizers, simply by the use of consciousness?

We have been teaching people for 30 years how to use Radionics, such as using the SE-5, which is utilizing scalar technology to transport information to plants for example, so that they can grow without the use of fertilizers.

All the stories I have shared where either Don and I or others have created miracles, small or large in their life, have been based on learning how to navigate the realms of consciousness.

The *Living From Vision®* course and *Holodynamics,* the art of transforming the negative into its positive counterpart and thereby shapeshifting time and space are the tools that everyone can utilize to create a better world for themselves and the planet.

Join me on a journey to creating a better life for yourself and the planet and take the first step today.

I am offering a FREE APP to start out your day right and end your day on a good note: LFV LITE for Apple and Android on www.ilonaselke.com

Now let me take you to a final view of what is possible as we awaken in a larger numbers – The Global Brain.

GLOBAL SHIFTSAND THE GLOBAL MIND

What do you think? Can our imagination shift global events? Or do you feel that we are each working alone by ourselves? Or, can we make a change if enough of us hold a vision together? Are we having a collective influence?

Are we already working as one global mind together without knowing it?

Decades ago, in 1982, the concept of The Global Brain had been postulated by Peter Russelllong before the Internet had been formed.

He told us that a living being is made up of many organs. Each organ is a burgeoning bunch of cells before it becomes a new organ. Yet miraculously, when the mass of about 10 billion cells is reached, this mass becomes a new organ.

He foresaw the time when humans would reach the 10 billion mark. When that happens and you must remember that at that time we only had 4.2 billion humans on the planet, but once reaching the 10 billion benchmark, we would enter a new phase of being human. We would create a new organism. He called it the **Global Brain.** Peter Russell based his theory on observing evolution over billions of years.

In the primal soup we didn't even have single-celled beings. Eventually the single cells evolved and at the juncture of about 10,000,000,000 cells (10 billon), a hyper jump appeared and these 10,000,000,000 cells formed a new unit, a new organ or organism.

When I heard about his work decades ago, I never ever fathomed that the Global Brain might be technologically induced. I was curious as to how his theory, which I felt had some merit, would manifest.

Decades later, with almost 7.5 billion humans on this planet, we are nearing his benchmark for a new organism. I am not sure how this will look, but we might already be seeing the gestalt of the new Global Brain in the making.

Quoting from his website: "The Internet is linking humanity into one worldwide community – a "global brain". This, combined with a rapidly growing spiritual awakening, is creating a collective consciousness that is humanity's only hope of saving itself from itself." However, Russell warns, "if we continue on our current path of greed and destruction, humanity will become a planetary cancer."

Selling more than 100,000 copies and translated into ten languages, his seminal work, *The Global Brain*, won acclaim from forward thinkers worldwide. It was regarded by many as years ahead of its time, and its original predictions about the impact of computer networks and changing social values are now being realized.

Peter Russell, who holds advanced degrees in theoretical physics, experimental psychology and computer science, makes no apologies for presenting what may seem like a Utopian theory.

And here I find the greatest prophetic message he can give us.

He advises, "The image a society has of itself can play a crucial role in the shaping of its future. A positive vision is like the light at the end of the tunnel, which, even though dimly glimpsed, encourages us to step in that direction."

We are, by and large, already globally interconnected via the Internet. We are able to share visions, passions, dreams, and uplift each other by the billions.

However, that which sells best seems to be the shocking, scary, and the horrible news. Yes, we do need to be informed in order to know what the current issues are in order to get to work and apply our mind and vision to create a better future. But it does require that we realize that we are very potent co-creators.

Luckily, through mass media, books and the internet, we can share our vision and solutions. These positive inspirations and inventions can spread like wildfire through the interconnected Global Brain.

And this is what most people don't know – each of us is a dreamer of our collective dream.

Here is one way in which you can participate to create global positive changes:

Most people reading this far in the book either trust or already realize that we do create at least some changes in our world through our focus. Be it a parking space or the seeming coincidences, we do see the uncanny relationship between what we hold in our mind and what manifests around us.

The Big Secret is that what we can feel as a wish already

fulfilled, so much so that we can feel it down to our bones, that wish will usually manifest. Many people who are reading this book have already had experiences with manifesting. For many it is still a mystery and at times unpredictable. Learning the steps of how to manifest is part of what I have been teaching internationally for the last 30 years with the *Living From Vision®* course. In the process of learning the ABCs of manifesting, we become multidimensional beings.

Since we can apply the principles of elevated consciousness to our personal life, it stands to reason that we can also affect the global reality, individually and together.

When we realize that every solution we hold in our vision, in our heart and in our bones can come true, then the next step is to become global co-creators.

Let me tell you a story of how I applied the methods of transformation that I've explained in this book to affect global change.

It is a simple exercise that you can do by yourself weekly and become a positive change maker for this planet:

Living in Bali and running our Shambala Retreat Center, I was faced with the rude awakening that Bali had been catapulted into the Western world, with all its plastic, in a hurry. Just a few decades earlier, there had been no plastic on the island of Bali. Now however, every little thing is wrapped in plastic. The Bali people disposed of it like they have always done in the past when everything was still wrapped in banana leaves.

They threw it away into nature or piled it up and burned it. They even have special burning days, coordinated communally, across the island to get rid of their trash.

Plastic therefore started to accumulate in the river beds and was taken out to the ocean during heavy rainfall. The rivers act like great conveyor belts. Since we are living right by the ocean we are witness to the trash that comes rushing down the river bed next to our center.

Most of us have a neat trashcan that we set out onto the street side and have it picked up with trucks to have it transported away. It's out of sight and out of mind. Such luxury of trash pick-up does not exist in the rural parts of the world.

Watching the plastic wash into the ocean was a horror to behold. We started picking up the trash from the riverbed as it piled up onto the last 200 yards prior to emptying into the ocean. Of course that reduced the amount of trash emptying into the ocean.

It was not only Bali, but until not so long ago, New York tossed all its garbage out to the sea. Through most of its history until the mid-1900s, New York's primary method for disposing of its waste was simply to dump it into the ocean. At one point, as much as 80% of New York's garbage ended up out at sea. [The Guardian, US Edition, 27. Oct. 2016]

Plastic is a huge issue currently and in my heart of hearts, I wanted to find a more global solution to plastic.

Here's what I did:

Every weekend, on Saturdays, I sat for about 5 to 15

minutes in silence and daydreamed that I was living in a future, already now, where we had discovered a microbe that was able to break down the plastic into natural compounds and could return the plastic to the earth.

I simply fast-forwarded myself into the future (already fulfilled), where the solution already existed.

Each week for those short moments, I held in my inner mind a world in which the discovery of something that could digest plastic into its natural components had already been discovered.

I could literally feel that I had arrived in a world where plastic was no longer a threat to the environment but instead, where plastic could be decomposed into its organic components.

It can be difficult to imagine a world in which something that doesn't currently exist, has already been invented and already exists. It takes practice to see the not-yet-manifest, as if it is manifest. It is an art. Keeping the proverbial balance and remain sane takes a keen mind and soul.

Simultaneously knowing what is and what will be, as if it is now already true. This stretch is a multidimensional surfing stunt and should be practiced carefully. For example, I do not promote the use of a credit card for advance cash, because the money sure is coming real soon now.

Feel the reality as if it has manifested and wait for the proof! It can happen quickly, or it can take time. But the proof in this dimension will ensure you are in balance and at the right time at the right place.

And let us remember, it is always a co-creative process! If we ask that all our wishes are manifested for the highest good, and can be either supported or ameliorated by "the universe" or whatever you wish to call the "higher force", our ego is taken out of the game.

This means that we instruct the global hologram with our vision and the universal power actualizes this vision in accordance to a higher plan. This can work because you are an individualized diamond or drop of the entire ocean called IT, God, or the entire field of consciousness.

As such, you ARE PART OF THE WHOLE. What goes on inside of you will sooner or later go on outside of you. As above, so below. As within, so without.

What we live in is a multidimensional, multi-layered hologram which has one source-code and is externalized into many parts all sharing that same source-code.

When you activate heightened awareness inside your core, your soul's essence, and focalize your intensity of awareness, then you automatically start vibrating at a higher frequency which in turn can embrace greater fields of time-space.

I want to postulate that when you focus yourself at a heightened state, into a state of being that embraces more intensity of is-ness within yourself, then when you are day-dreaming of a "may-be-world", you are dialing into a future that is available as one of the many parallel realities. That is how the rishis, prophets,seers and yogis can access information from the past and the future

This type of daydreaming has to be accompanied with an inner certainty which happens when you hit on the correct frequency. Your feeling, vision and core beliefs all have to align.

This alignment of yourself with a greater, positive future can be visual. But more often than not it is a felt sense of "clicking" into the fulfilled future. It's a subtle shift from being in the current problem world to the solution world. But when you can make that shift, either for a personal issue or a global issue, it is a real shift and it will become manifest. It is an art to develop this ability.

It is almost like you're dialing into a future parallel expression of a potential of your choice once you dive into this future, with the desirable outcome.

Can you believe it? One year later I actually heard the GREAT NEWS.

First a group of Yale University students had discovered a fungus that could digest plastic. They had discovered an anaerobic fungus that is able to decompose plastic into its organic components.

A couple of years later, a Japanese team of researchers,Shosuke Yoshida*et al.,* discovered a bacteria that degrades and assimilates poly(ethylene terephthalate) as it states in the article by SCIENCE on 03/11/2016.

That is when I felt I had done my share of dreaming a solution into existence. Did my dreaming assist in this process or was it just coincidence?

We do know from the research of Dr. Emoto that thoughts are able to affect molecular change at a distance of water drops that were frozen and analyzed under a microscope.

The two experiments that stand out to me are the following:

First, Emoto took a water vial and had 500 people send prayers to it from a long distance away. The crystallization of the water after the prayers had been projected onto it and frozen showed a sizable improvement when placed under a microscope. The crystallization was dramatically more complex and organized compared to the original water.

Second, he took water from a lake before and after a monk had blessed the water of the lake. The difference of the crystallization of the water before and after his blessing were even more stunning. And, mind you, the sample was taken from a vast lake, not just one small vial. The complexity and beauty far surpassed the design created by the 500 meditators. It only took one trained, focused person to create a greater result.

This means that it does not necessarily take a vast amount of minds and souls to focus together to create change. The changes can be achieved by the higher purity and focus of one individual as well.

Our scientific model of the universe does not have a clear model as to what stuff our reality is made of. Science does not know what the substratum of our reality really is. What we consider reality maybe a hyper-dimensional quantum foam that blinks into existence and is, in fact, not as solid as we think. But we have more and more scientists considering that we are living in a Consciousness Interactive Universe. Some are postulating that we live in a gigantic hologram.

Whatever this reality is, one thing is for sure. THE UNIVERSE IS LISTENING. TO EACH AND EVERY ONE OF US. We know this from the many anomalous stories of science defying achievements and miracles.

We do know that what differentiates some of the thoughts manifesting more quickly and easily versus more slowly depends utterly on the fact that we FOCUS our awareness. And we know that it depends on the locus of our soul awareness, meaning the height (if you were to give special definition to "lower" and "higher" frequencies.)

The higher we are focused within our own self, the higher we vibrate to begin with, the more potent our focus is. End of story. Let us say, you have your locus of soul awareness at a level where we have our planet's stratosphere. You can imagine that you would have a greater outreach much like an umbrella that encompasses greater time-space.

As we realize more and more that we are co-creating a reality from within our own consciousness, we are more and more inclined to envision positive, holistic, all-encompassing thoughts and feelings.

I hope that you will start having your weekly global dreaming sessions, in which you step into a fulfilled future in which solutions have been already discovered.

As you are vibrating that future into the very core of your now state, that discovery will come into the very now that you occupy.

I was so excited to read such great news after one year of having my weekly global solution sessions.

Each year that followed brought more breakthroughs. I am currently holding the vision that this and other innovative achievements will be utilized worldwide and transform our plastic issue into an issue of the past.

I also worked on local solutions and smaller step by step solutions. On the home front in Bali, we had meetings with the mayor of the town, came up with slogans for the youth groups and went to schools and distributed books which taught over a three months' time period on how to recycle and compost trash.

With the help of a forward thinking mayor in Bondalem where our *Shambala Retreat* is located, we were allowed to be accepted into several local schools where we could pay teachers to teach the curriculum of how to compost and recycle.

One seminar participant of mine, a woman from Switzerland was a previous trainer in the military of Switzerland. She helped us make some of these dreams come true. Upon attending one of our seminars in Bali, she was so inspired by our efforts that she collected a larger sum of money through the LIONS CLUB and donated these funds to our effort of managing the plastic trash issue in Bondalem. These funds helped pay teachers to teach school sessions to the children of the second grade through the fifth grade. What is taught in school goes home. What children read in textbooks, they believe in! And who knows, the next mayor in a decade or two of this town may well come from one of those classes and remember the importance of recycling and waste management.

Dreaming big, to create a better world for yourself and the planet, is a way to ascend to a greater human being. Learning how to raise one's consciousness to be able to affect time space more effectively is the carrot that creation has given us. As we raise our vibration, our lives become more beautiful and we become increasingly able to sit at the steering wheel of our life.

COLLECTIVE NAVIGATION

There is yet another kind of Global Brain I had in mind.

Here is an experiment that proves how all our minds are capable and already are cooperating to work together as a whole, whether we are consciously aware of it or not. The result will most likely astound you. And I hope it will make you be more attentive to the kind of future you envision.

Do you live in the world where you think the Earth is going downhill? Do you think our future generations have a chance? Do you envision a more beautiful future which future generations will inherit from us?

We are indeed working together as one whole unit of consciousness to create change collectively, as you can see demonstrated in this experiment.

An article titled *Das Lebewesen Menschheit*, written in **the P.M. Magazine** published in January 2005, page 45, described an amazing experiment. The question that was posed was the following: Are 5000 laypeople able to steer an airplane together?

I'm sure you would agree with me that that would be hard to imagine. However, in an auditorium in Las Vegas, researchers created a scenario that proves that our minds work as a unit, even when we don't talk with each other.

5000 enthusiastic people sitting in an auditorium in Las Vegas were given a piece of cardboard which was red on one side and green on the other side. Cameras were installed in the ceiling of the auditorium that could read the color that the audience was asked to show to the cameras. Each person had the choice to flip the cardboard so that either the color red or the color green showed toward the ceiling.

The cameras that were located in the four quadrants of the hall above the audience were connected to a flight simulator. The cockpit of an airplane was projected onto the screen in the auditorium. Everybody in the hall was able to see the view from the cockpit projected onto the big screen and thereby everybody was virtually turned into a small part of a conglomerate pilot. One out of 5000 pilots.

You know the saying that too many cooks disturb the pie. Well, this story was going to prove something very unimaginable.

The steering mechanism of the flight simulator was determined by the relationship and location between the red and the green cards. The right side of the hall was representative of the rudder that determines the height of the airplane, and the left side of the hall was controlling the ability for the airplane to turn.

No one single person was directing the airplane. It was the collective whole that directed the flight.

To start out, the researchers had the airplane flying at a great height. Down below we see a small landing strip. That's where this airplane is supposed to land.

The airplane sways to the left and right. "Red, red, more red a number of people were shouting from the right side of the hall while they are holding up the red side of the cardboard cards towards the camera. "More green" somebody is shouting from another corner of the auditorium. The airplane tumbles and everybody in the auditorium is holding their breath, hissing and moaning.

Just as everybody expected the end, somehow the airplane was pulled up by the right mixture of green and red cards in the auditorium. Nothing that one single person had decided. Everybody had collaborated.

The airplane pulls a great loop and stabilizes. As if everybody had been talking together out loud, you could almost hear the question hanging in the hall: "Can we bring this airplane to fly a loop?"

It was a collective thought, a collective question. The airplane climbs, flips, and the simulated airplane catches itself. Everybody is excited. They had just flown a loop as a collective. Everybody is touched beyond measure. Something had happened in the collective consciousness and an ability had become realized that not one single person could've accomplished. But it was accomplished by the ONE MIND.

The individuals of this group became one unit and became part of a greater task. They became part of something that started to function to the tunes of a higher order.

Numerous scientists have already postulated that our individual consciousness will be united together to become one super organism. Dr. Gregory Stark calls it the

Meta-human. The Meta-human is a unity out of everything that was humanly created. Everything that belongs to what makes a human.

We can certainly see the advent of this meta-consciousness becoming more pronounced around the globe through the advent of technology. Artificial intelligence, AI is in the process of becoming such a meta-structure. Peter Russell proposed the Global Brain and the advent of the Internet is showing such an outward form of a unified consciousness.

But the experiment of flying an airplane collectively is pointing to a much greater meta-consciousness. This field of one mind is involving humans and other beings working together in unison, unified in an invisible dimension where our collective dreams create collective solutions.

We are already doing this together. Long before the days when faxes existed, I was puzzled how it was possible that so many people from around the world could send us checks in the mail to order a particular item from us, on the exact same day for the same item. How were they talking together?

We are part of a wave function and often don't realize that we already act in unison or as if directed from a level of wholeness that is beyond the level of rational reasoning.

However, that kind of mind in action at a distance is not that well known to the mainstream. It has been researched by government forces, yet kept hidden from the masses. It has even been ridiculed. Understanding action at a distance or non-local causality can only be understood when you have a world model that includes a higher substratum of an organizing field that allows for what otherwise appears as an impossible coincidence.

"Wherever two or more unite, there I will be amongst them," is what Jesus said. He hinted that the fact that when we unite our consciousness in a higher vibratory place of unity, such as believing in one higher force, the higher force will be invited and be amongst the ones who focus on it.

10 billion cells unite to become a new organ. 10 billion minds working as one unit become a meta-mind, with or without the internet.

It is my feeling that we will be able to each operate at a true META-MIND when we tap into a higher frequency dimension. That is why I just told you about the example of flying the simulated airplane with a group of 5000 people in the hall without much communication.

When each of us is able to activate the locus of our consciousness at this higher dimension, we will collectively encompass a much larger time-space configuration in the 3-D world. That is when we will collectively enter into fourth dimensional living.

Much like the picture in my earlier chapter The Art of Union of Souls, when I showed two human beings focusing together into a singularity, we can all start to operate this Inner-Net and create a healthier future for ourselves here on this planet.

We don't have to wait until all humans on this planet are able to do so. Just like reading and writing was not commonplace just a couple of hundred years ago, slowly but surely it has become the dominant ability on this planet.

Our collective dreaming, either consciously or sub-consciously, determines our outcomes. Let us start by dreaming big, consciously, and clean up our subconscious beliefs and fears.

As you read in earlier chapters, we need to purify our focus on all levels to have positive effects.

Once we become aware of the problem, for example too much plastic trash, we can become proactive and begin to envision the fulfilled future in which a solution has already been offered.

That is when we become not only the change agent in our personal lives but that is when we then become ACTIVE AGENTS OF CHANGE HERE ON EARTH for the greater whole.

CO-CREATING or EGO-CREATING

The YES you feel in your heart and bones is the resounding yes that the universe gives you, as it replies to your request. When you are able to sense the positive RESPONSE BACK from the universe, which is an ability you will learn with practice, then you know you are on the right path.

In utilizing the higher dimensions to create something, you are actually co-creating your vision with the higher support of the universe.

There is much confusion about how being spiritual and manifesting goes together. These two paths are often seen to be polar opposites. Often manifesting gets confused with a willful, egoic way to get what one wants. We don't need to manifest to do that. We can just make enough money to buy anything that pleases us.

The ego has and can create anything, but usually at a price. Caesar stands as an icon for might, a might that comes from the egoic will.

But the egoic will is not as powerful as the power that comes from surrender to the greater whole, to the co-creation of the universe.

In order to manifest, we need to learn the ABCs of reality. Thoughts and feelings that we hold in our conscious as well as subconscious mind, all matter.

The more separated we feel, the less power we have. The more we are able to truly rise to a greater field and unite with it, we increase our power. But that power no longer sees the "me" as winning over the "you". It does not get something at the expense of someone else, or something. It does not even get what it wants but rather starts to rely more and more on a magical co-creative dance of the whole and the part, dancing together.

The universe is always listening to the very nuances of our thoughts and feelings. We are united with that field, the source in every cell of our being. This greater field can be our source of true power and also double check on our requests to ensure that we are co-creating with a higher, wiser perspective. I like calling it **co-creating with God.**

And you can apply this to global issues as well as personal issues.

EPILOGUE

THE ULTIMATE DREAM – AWAKENING

As I am finishing my book on the eve of the solar eclipse August 21, 2017, I am awed at the timing. Tomorrow morning we will be able to see the eclipse here from our island home in the Pacific Northwest more than 90%. Having lived in Bali, I have become even more sensitive to timing. In Bali, people live by the cosmic calendar and I smile at the cosmic timing for the ending of my book as I am writing the final pages here tonight. Many times I had wanted the process to go faster, but there is something that is divinely guided if we but listen.

I started this book by telling you about my early beginnings in the Himalayas and later about my childhood ideals. In retrospect I can say now that I had been majorly inspired by the movie *"I Dream of Jeannie"* and the fairy tale of 1001 Nights, *"Aladdin"*, as well as the adventures of the TV dolphin by the name of *"Flipper"*.

In my teenage years I was mesmerized by the tale of *Siddhartha* and stories of the yogis and seers from the Far East in the book *Autobiography of a Yogi*, by ParamahansaYogananda and finally *The Lazy Man's Guide to Enlightenment* by Thaddeus Golas.

These books and tales about magic and enlightenment have served as the golden thread that flowed throughout my life and have accompanied me to this very day. Even the décor at our homes around the world and our *Shambala*

<u>Retreat Center</u> in Bali reflect my visions and fancies which I had as a child and teenager.

First, I mention this because I want to encourage you to become more aware of the stories that motivated you in your childhood. Remember back to the stories that were important to you back then. Look for the golden thread in your life and see how your deepest fascinations have manifested around you. This thread can give you many clues and pointers as to what you may still want to explore.

Second, I want to point out how important it is that we carefully feed the minds of our children. Not only will the food and what they eat determine who they become, but what we feed their minds, hearts and souls will also determine who and what they become.

Many children are put into the hands of teachers from an early age, people who can't give them the amount of attention, hugs and love that parents can give. Listen to your children and assume they have lived before. They are coming in with a certain amount of wisdom already and a desire to learn certain things. Listen to their wisdom and attend to their needs.

Beyond that, practice listening to your own heart and soul. Do that every day! Start your day right and end your day on a good note by doing some kind of meditation.

Gratitude and seeing beauty are two very reliable methods to ensure that you raise your vibration.

To that end I am gifting you the Dream Big APP so you can set your vision, your heart and mind on a path of a higher octave.

To download the Dream Big APP for FREE please go to my Homepage www.ilonaselke.com and sign up for the Dream Big APP. That way you can start your day right and end your day on a good note. Doing daily imagery exercises like the ones I provide in the Dream Big APP is a great way to create miracles in your daily life.

If you wish to dive into practicing Living From Vision for yourself or become an LFV-coach, or teach LFV in classes, please go to www.livingfromvision.com

The images we hold, whether consciously or subconsciously, influence our reality all the time.

Pay attention to what you let into your mind.

Remember to REFOCUS on what you want if things are not going as you wish.

Practice to step out of the "movie" called life and become the observer for a moment.

This very brief moment allows you to get in touch with your higher perspective, with your soul.

The truths of the scientific community are only half-truths. Our Western mind, steeped in the scientific model, has largely been occupied with the world of appearances.

This outward focus has led us down a potentially negative path. Instead of focusing on telepathy, we rely on phones. Instead of accessing the Akashic Records, we have the internet. Instead of friends and counselors we will soon have AI (artificial intelligence) chat Bots.

The eastern world long occupied itself with development of virtues, the discovery of the hidden dimensions and the invisible worlds.

At a time when AI is about to take over the entire planet based on the values and beliefs of the Western mindset that puts the mind, logic and physicality above the higher dimensional mind, above intuition and even disregards the existence of soul, we are indeed at a crossroads of our human evolution.

The advent of Artificial Intelligence poses a deeper threat to our humanness than currently can be understood.

Soul is what inhabits the physical body. By getting in touch with our soul first, the divine world will ensure greater ability to create a Heaven on Earth than what AI can ever promise. After all, what we take with us beyond the boundary of what we call death of the physical body, is precisely only those abilities that we have developed in our soul.

You can become the synthesis and the savior of your life by developing your soul's awareness and by discovering that consciousness and the many subtle dimensions of soul awareness are the real causative agent for what we experience in the physical world.

When you increasingly manifest what is in alignment with your soul, you will be aiding the development of the new *HomoDivinicus.*

We all need to feel that we are in the driver's seat of our life. By learning how to co-create, how to manifest consciously and how to express what is deeply

279

meaningful to you, you will naturally grow into your next level of evolution.

Our survival may depend on you making the link between the dreaming universe and the outer world of forms.

If this mystical knowledge were to disappear, AI may be the only survivor.

We are souls incarnated in physical bodies and we are here to grow and learn and to become more filled with light and love. That is the purpose of life.

That is why we need every single one of us here on Earth to practice and practice and practice until we become masters of the dreamtime. With practice, we can become masters of soul awareness and will realize that we co-create with a much larger force.

God, the All – that – is, is equally interested in us discovering It, as we are interested in discovering It.

With The Source, or God, or whatever you call the higher force of the universe as the **co-creator by your side**, you can be sure that whatever your greatest dreams are, they will be fueled by a source and power much greater than your individual self could ever muster up.

This greater source is awaiting our return.

In the process of becoming conscious co-creators, we awaken continuously more and more to the ultimate awakening, that we are ONE with ALL – THAT – IS.

The **LIVING FROM VISION** ONLINE COURSE

For MORE INFORMATION please go to:

www.livingfromvision.com

LFV-Online Course

LFV-Coaching

LFV-Coach-Training

LFV Teacher Training

BONUS:

www.ilonaselke.com

To claim your FREE BONUS

The Dream Big APP!

Ilona Selke
For more information about music, guided meditations,
webinars, and books by Ilona Selke go to
www.ilonaselke.com

Ilona Selke

CPSIA information can be obtained
at www.ICGtesting.com
Printed in the USA
FSOW03n1849260917
39015FS